Bernhard Felsenthal, Herman Eliassof

History of Kehillath Anshe Maarabh

Congregation of the Men of the West

Bernhard Felsenthal, Herman Eliassof

History of Kehillath Anshe Maarabh
Congregation of the Men of the West

ISBN/EAN: 9783744795784

Printed in Europe, USA, Canada, Australia, Japan

Cover: Foto ©ninafisch / pixelio.de

More available books at **www.hansebooks.com**

HISTORY OF

Kehillath Anshe Maarabh

(Congregation of the Men of the West)

ISSUED UNDER THE AUSPICES OF THE CONGREGATION
ON THE OCCASION OF ITS

SEMI-CENTENNIAL CELEBRATION,

NOVEMBER 4, 1897.

—

BY DR. B. FELSENTHAL AND HERMAN ELIASSOF.

— — ———— —

CHICAGO,

1897.

CONTENTS.

INTRODUCTORY.

EVERYWHERE among civilized people it is considered meet and proper that anniversaries be celebrated. Such celebrations, if they are conducted in the proper manner, have a deeper meaning and a higher import than is usually supposed. For they are apt to recall to our memory events of the past and to put before our mind the questions: What results have been achieved thus far? What aims have been reached? What progress has been made?

Such celebrations may, in addition, direct our thoughts more earnestly towards examining present conditions, and they may lead us to reflect what might be the proper course to pursue hereafter, and what particular action would be required in order to reach still higher aims and purposes. And reflections of this kind —may they not prove to be of the highest moral and material consequences?

קְהִלַּת אַנְשֵׁי מַעֲרָב (Kehillath Anshe Maarabh Congregation of the Men of the West) now looks upon a history of fifty years, and celebrates its Semi-Centennial.

Said Kehillath Anshe Maarabh is the oldest Jewish congregation in Chicago, in fact in all the Northwestern States of our country. At the time it was organized (1847) it was of all the then existing congregations in the United States the one which had been established so far in the West; hence its name: "Congregation

5

of the Men of the West." It has had a blissful influence not only upon those who have been immediately
connected with it as members or otherwise, but also,
indirectly, upon wider circles. It has been a source of
religious blessing for many who sleep now in their
silent graves, and for many who are still with us. And
we hope also that in the future K. A. M. will remain a
power, working for religious and moral uplifting of the
people and for the glory of our Jewish religion; we
hope that in coming times, too, it may prosper and
flourish and be one of the foremost Jewish congregations in our blessed country.

This historical monograph is issued by Congregation
"*Kehillath Anshe Maarabh*," on the occasion of the
celebration of its Golden Jubilee, as a souvenir for its
members and their friends, in commemoration of the
good work of the pioneers of the Jewish community of
Chicago, who, in their true religious hearts and their
faithful adherence to Judaism, braved every obstacle
and shunned no sacrifice in order to gain a permanent
footing for, and to secure the future of Israel's religion
in the then remote corner of the western wilds of our
broad land.

The history of the origin of K. A. M., the mother
of many of our organizations of to-day, discloses to
view an important period of the past. In the open
vista appears the vivid picture of half a century of
Jewish life in Chicago, which must engross the deepest interest of a great number of our Jewish citizens.
Many descendants, relations and friends of the old settlers, whose names are mentioned here, are still living
in our midst. The dear faces of the beloved ones, who
have long ago departed from amongst the living, smile
once again from these pages, and the account of their

noble deeds must fill the hearts of their descendants
with just pride, and awaken in them the most tender
memories. For, the heroic devotion of the founders of
the congregation to Judaism, their deep reverence and
burning enthusiasm for the cause of Israel, invite the
world's unstinted admiration.

The founders of the congregation are now all but
one (may God prolong his noble life) resting in the
realms of eternity. In profound gratitude, K. A. M.
lays these leaves as wreaths upon their graves as a
token of respect. These wreaths are to serve as evidence that the memory of their good deeds is still
cherished by those who enjoy the fruit of their labors
of love—their indefatigable efforts for the perpetuation
of Judaism.

I.

THE PAST.

–

ORIGIN OF THE CHICAGO JEWISH
COMMUNITY.

EFORE proceeding to the history of the
congregation proper, it may not be out
of place to make some statements here
concerning the earliest history of the Jews
in Chicago in general.

The city of Chicago, which is now counted among
the largest and most populous cities of the world, is,
so to say, of recent origin. It received its charter as
a city not earlier than the year 1837, and in that year
its first mayor was elected. But how wonderfully has
it grown during the comparatively short period of sixty
years which since then has elapsed! Indeed, the story
of Chicago's growth reads like a fairy tale.

It is possible and likely that already in the very first
years of Chicago's existence as a city, and perhaps
even prior to 1837, a few individual Jews may have
come to this part of America. But if so, they must
soon have left the town again. No living man's memory knows anything about them; in none of the
records which we could examine could we find a trace
of them. The first authentic information about Jews

9

coming to Chicago and settling here does not go farther
back than the year 1841.

To the Eastern States, especially to the great cities
on the Atlantic seashore, to New York, Philadelphia
and Baltimore, large numbers of German Jews had come
between 1830 and 1840. In that period most of them
hailed from Bavaria and from the Rhenish Palatinate.
They came from beyond the Atlantic, expecting to find
in the United States not only better prospects in their
various pursuits of life, but also equal rights, instead of
offensive and exclusive laws under which the Jews still
had to suffer at that time in the old Fatherland. Here,
in the United States, they found a new Fatherland,
granting them full civil and political rights, equally
with the citizens of other denominations. And these
new-comers, confessing the old Jewish faith, appreciated
this, and warm and sincere was their thankful attach-
ment to their new country.

Very soon a considerable number of the Jewish im-
migrants found their way to the Valley of the Ohio and
to the Prairies of the West. And, as said above, a
larger number of Jews came to Chicago in the year
1843.

Previous to 1845 there was no religious organization
among the Jews in Chicago, nor were there many Jews
in Chicago or even Illinois before 1840. The strong
tide of Jewish immigration commenced after the com-
pletion of the Illinois & Michigan Canal, and of the
Galena & Chicago R. R. to Elgin, in 1849. At that
time Chicago became a center of trade attracting Jewish
families as permanent settlers. Prior to this important
event in the history of Chicago, there had been residing
in this city but two Jewish families, one of them being
that of Benedict Schubert, who came here in 1841, and

the other that of Philip Neuburg.   Mr. Schubert had become quite wealthy.   It was he—according to the statement of one of the oldest Jewish settlers here—who was among the first for whom a brick house was erected on Lake Street, where he carried on his business.   He had been a tailor, and by his industry he soon acquired sufficient means, and became, in his day, one of the leading merchant tailors in Chicago.   His son, Aaron Schubert, is living in Chicago to-day.

The first Jew to buy land in Cook County, to live on it as a farmer, was Mr. Henry Meyer, who came to Illinois in the spring of 1847.   He bought of the government 160 acres, situated in the town of Schaumburg, Cook County, where he remained until he became advanced in years, and, being without grown children, he removed to Chicago.   He had sold his farm and invested all his funds in Chicago real estate.   As a far-seeing man of sound judgment in such matters, he advised his friends and acquaintances to act similarly; he desired that they should do so, with at least a part of their means.   Time proved that he was right. Though his investment brought no immediate fruits to himself, yet to those who followed his example and bought land it became a rich mine of wealth.

Chicago had meanwhile become widely known, and many Israelites were induced to select this place as their home.   Among the first ones, who about that time came to Chicago, were: Isaac Ziegler, Levi Rosenfeld, Jacob Rosenberg, the brothers Kohn (Abraham, Hirsch and Moses), Samuel Cole, M. M. Gerstley, the brothers Rubel, the brothers Greenebaum, Louis Mayer, Max L. Mayer, Morris L. Leopold, M. Braunschild, Jacob Fuller, Max Weineman, B. Bruneman, M.Weigselbaum, Martin Clayburgh, Isaac Wormser, Leon Greenebaum and brothers, M. Becker,* Isaac Engle. B. Stern, A. Frank, Isaac Wolf, Marcus Peiser and others.

On the Day of Atonement, 1845, religious services were held for the first time in the Jewish community of Chicago. The temporary congregation met in a private room above a store on Wells Street, now Fifth Avenue. The following persons were present: Benedict Schubert, Jacob Rosenberg,** S. Friedheim, who lived at Pigeon Woods, west of Elgin, Ill.; the brothers Judas, Abraham, Morris and Mayer Kohn, Harry Benjamin, and Isaac Ziegler. As but a *minyan* (ten male adults, the requisite number for public worship) was present, the services had to be discontinued whenever one of the congregation left the room, and the assembly had to wait until the absent member returned. Mr. Neuburg and Mayer L. Klein officiated as *Hazzanim*, or readers, at these services.

The second public services were held on Yom Kippur. 1846, also in a private room, above the store of Messrs. Rosenfeld & Rosenberg, 155 Lake Street. The cantors on this occasion were Philip Neuburg and Abraham Kohn. Not many more persons were present at this service than at the first. The brothers Kohn, mentioned above, brought along a Sepher Torah (scroll of the Law) from Germany, when they came to America, and this sepher was used at both services.

In 1845 the first Jewish organization was established under the name of "Jewish Burial Ground Society." The first public act by which the Jews of Chicago demonstrated their existence as a body corporate was the purchase from the city of one acre of ground for a

---

* These two went together to San Francisco, California, in 1849, and found their untimely death there, having perished in the fire that visited that city in 1851.

** His partner, Levi Rosenfeld, was absent from the city.

cemetery, for which they paid $46. This parcel of ground was located on the North Side, now within the confines of Lincoln Park. This old Jewish cemetery had to be abandoned as a burial place in 1857, the city having become meanwhile so extensive that the cemetery was within the city limits.

Not exactly a congregation, but a society of a semi-religious character, was instituted in 1851 by a number of young Israelites in Chicago, under the name of *Hebrew Benevolent Society*. It purchased three acres of ground in the town of Lake View, a little south of Graceland Cemetery, and laid it out as a burial ground. The Jewish Burial Ground Society did not exist very long, but the Hebrew Benevolent Society is still in existence to-day and still owns its burial ground in Graceland, next to B'nai Sholom Cemetery. Following are the names of the charter members of the Hebrew Benevolent Society: Moses Rubel, Michael Greenebaum, Mayer L. Klein, Elias Greenebaum, Levi Klein, and Isaac Wolf. Michael Greenebaum was elected the first President.

KEHILATH ANSHE MAYRIV.

HE records of K. A. M., covering the period from the close of 1847 (the time of its formation) to that of 1871, were entirely destroyed in the Chicago fire, and so were all other documents, bearing upon the history of the Chicago Jewish community written prior to the conflagration, consumed by this raging element. About thirty years ago Dr. B. Felsenthal deposited with the Chicago Historical Society a document treating upon the general history of the Jews of Chicago. This paper met with the same fate as the rest of the property of the society. On the occasion of the dedication of the K. A. M. Temple, corner Peck Court and Wabash Avenue, in 1868, the late Mr. M. M. Gerstley, who was president of K. A. M. from 1861 to 1891, compiled a record of the early history of the Chicago Jewish community, and this valuable document was burned in the second fire of July, 1874. In writing the history of the genesis of K. A. M., we are therefore compelled to rely entirely upon oral statements of old Jewish settlers and information gleaned here and there from old newspaper articles, and other unauthentic sources.

Errors and omissions can hardly be avoided under the existing circumstances, and the writers of this work proceed with the history of K. A. M. in the hope that the reader will take into consideration the above statement of facts and not judge their work too severely.

The tide of immigration continued to flow westward

with increasing vigor.   The population of Chicago was
daily growing larger, and the Jewish community, too.
became numerically stronger.   Soon the desire to estab-
lish a congregation manifested itself.   The leaders of
the Jewish community met to discuss the question, and
they decided that the number of co-religionists was yet
too limited to support two separate institutions, a Burial
Ground Society and a congregation.   But the members
of the Burial Ground Society were very anxious to have
a congregation established, and they resolved to aid in
the organization of such an institution.   On the third
day of November, 1847, a small body of co-religionists,
not exceeding twenty in number, assembled in the dry
goods store of Rosenfeld & Rosenberg, 155 Lake Street,
and formed a congregation under the name of "*K'chi-
lath Anshe Mayriv*,"*) the first Jewish congregation
in the great Northwest.   The Burial Ground Society
turned over its property to the new congregation and
finally ceased to exist.   On the next day, November
4th, the proposed constitution was adopted and signed
by the following fourteen members:

Abraham Kohn,	Levi Rosenfeld,
Jacob Rosenberg,	Jacob Fuller,
Samuel Cole,	M. Becker,
Morris L. Leopold,	Isaac Wormser.
Philip Neuburg,	B. Stern,
Benedict Schubert,	M. Braunschild,
Leon Greenebaum.	Judas Kohn.

The first election of officers resulted as follows:

---

* In transcribing the Hebrew קהלה אנשי מיערב somebody made
the mistake of rendering it "*Kehilath Anshe Mayriv*," instead of "*Kehillath
Anshe Maarabh*," meaning "Congregation of the Men of the West."   The
charter was obtained for that misspelled English name, which is the legal
title of congregation K. A. M. to the present day.   We use the incorporated
name wherever it is unavoidable, otherwise we render the correct paraphrase.

President—Morris L. Leopold.

Vice President and Treasurer—Abraham Kohn.

Secretary—Philip Neuburg.

Trustees—Benedict Schubert, Levi Rosenfeld and Leon Greenebaum.

Morris L. Leopold, the first President of K. A. M., was at the time of his election a young man of 26 years. He was born in Laubheim, Wurtemberg, April 10, 1821, and came to America in 1839, being then in his nineteenth year. In 1845 he married Rose Goodheart of Cincinnati, Ohio, and in the same year he moved to Chicago. In 1851 he returned to Cincinnati, where he remained until 1867, and then moved to New York, where he resided until his death, October 22, 1889. His widow still resides in New York.

At the time the congregation was founded Minhag Ashkenaz was adopted as the ritual for the synagogue. In the course of time demands became loud for having some reforms introduced into the service. Gradually a few such reforms were adopted, for instance, the abolition of the ritual of Piyutim and Selichoth, singing of hymns in the vernacular of the country, the accompanying of the singing by playing the organ, and a few other slight reforms.

In the spring of 1847 there came to Chicago an elderly Jewish lady of the name of Dila Kohn, *nee* Hirsch, with two of her sons and her daughter Clara. She had six sons, and four of these preceded her some four years. Tradition among the old Jewish settlers of Chicago ascribes to Mrs. Kohn the honor of having played an important part in the movement which was started in that year tending toward the formation of K. A. M. There was no *shochet* in the community. Mrs. Dila Kohn positively would eat no *trepha,* and she subsisted for a time on a vegetable diet, eating only bread, potatoes, eggs and the like. Her devoted sons would not permit this state of affairs to continue and began to agitate the organization of a congregation. The congregation was soon established, and Mrs. Kohn was the happiest woman in Chicago. Her son Abraham Kohn went to New York, and there made the acquaintance of Rev. Ignatz Kunreuther; he recommended him to the Chicago congregation, and Mr. Kunreuther was elected its Rabbi, reader and shochet.

Mrs. Dila Kohn was born in Gemnende, Bavaria, in 1793. Her parents died when she was very young, and the orphaned girl was brought up in the house of relatives in Wittelshofen, Bavaria. At the age of 15 she went to Italy, and lived in different families at Parma, Modena and Florence for a number of years. Returning to her native country, she was married in 1814 to Simon Joseph Kohn. In 1838 her husband died, and in 1847 Widow Kohn came to Chicago. She died here during the cholera epidemic of 1849. A son, Mayer Kohn, the last of her six sons, lives in Chicago to-day, and is still a member of K. A. M.

Rev. Ignatz Kunreuther, the first Rabbi of K. A. M., was born in the year 1811 at Gelnhausen, near Frankfort-on-the-Main. Although he was ultra orthodox in his views, holding tenaciously to ancient traditional usages, still he was not an intolerant man. He was a good Talmudic scholar and well versed in Hebrew literature. He also received instruction in secular knowledge. He was an unassuming, quiet and honest gentleman, and at all times ready to serve his fellow-men with acts of kindness. He was elected to the office November 5, 1847, and remained with his congregation for

MORRIS L. LEOPOLD.

about six years, from 1847 to 1853. On noticing the leaning of his congregation toward what he considered reform ideas, he severed his connection with K. A. M. and retired to private life. He was succeeded in office by Mr. Godfrey Snydacker as hazzan and teacher. Rabbi Kunreuther died in Chicago on the fourth day of Thammuz, 5644 (June 27, 1884), in the seventy-third year of his life. His widow and several daughters are living in this city to-day.

The first boy to get confirmed בר מצוה in a Chicago house of prayer was Julius Neuburg, son of Philip Neuburg. In January, 1851, he read his *parshah*, a portion of the Law, in the presence of the congregation. One week later Morris Barbe, whose father, Bernhard Barbe, was an active member of the congregation, assumed his religious responsibility in open meeting during public worship, and became בר מצוה These solemn acts took place in the room fitted up by the congregation for public worship, on Lake and Wells streets, over Harris & Summerfield's clothing store.

The first regular services of Congregation K. A. M. were held on the second floor of a building on the southwest corner of Lake and Wells streets, in a room which was appropriately fitted up as a synagogue. This room was soon found to be too small, and in 1849 the congregation leased a lot for five years on Clark Street, between Adams and Quincy, where the postoffice is now being built. Here a synagogue was to be erected.

This first synagogue of K. A. M., and the first Jewish house of worship in the State of Illinois, was dedicated on Friday, June 13, 1851. The auditorium was crowded to excess. The most influential citizens of Chicago were present, and several co-religionists traveled hundreds of miles in order to participate in the consecration. Rev. S. M. Isaacs of New York was the minister invited to deliver the dedicatory sermon. All the city papers teemed with paragraphs laudatory of his address. We quote from the *Daily Democrat's* report of the dedication:

No person that has made up his mind to be prejudiced against the Jews ought to have heard such a sermon preached. It was very captivating, and contained as much of real religion as any sermon we have ever heard preached. We never could have believed that one of these old Jews we have heard denounced so much could have taught so much liberality towards other denominations. The sermon was appropriate and eloquent, and was preached from the text: "They shall make unto me a sanctuary, so that I may dwell among them." The Jewish ladies cannot be beaten in decorating a place of worship. The flowers, leaves and bushes were woven into the most beautiful drapery that Chicago ever saw before.

The following hymn was sung at the dedication by a temporary choir to the tune of Old Hundred:

HYMN.

Be thou, O God, exalted high,
And as Thy glory fills the sky,
So let it be on earth display'd,
Till here on earth, as there, obey'd.

This temple to Thy hallow'd name
Is rais'd, Thy glory to proclaim;
Here we our sins' forgiveness crave,
Our hearts from secret pangs to save.

Vouchsafe this house Thy kind regard,
And to our prayers incline Thine ear:
O, let its founders meet reward,
And blessings its supporters cheer.

O grant that Israel soon may see
Jerusalem to its site restor'd;
When all men's hearts, from sin set free,
Shall sound Thy praise with one accord.

Mrs. DILA KOHN.

The congregation continued to prosper and to increase in membership.

The second President of K. A. M., from 1851 to
1853, was Levi Rosenfeld. He was born in Ditten-
heim, Bavaria, in 1816, came to America in 1839, and
to Chicago in 1843. In 1846 he married Miss Henriette Reese, in the city of New York. He always took
a great interest in the affairs of the congregation and
devoted much time and attention to its interests. He
was a plain, unassuming man, and remained so even
after he became very wealthy, of good business tact
and vast experience. His general knowledge of business matters was of great benefit to the congregation.
He died in Chicago in 1887. His esteemed wife, Mrs.
Henriette Rosenfeld, was a noble woman, and also a
true and faithful friend of K. A. M. She was very
charitable and a patron of many of the benevolent
institutions of Chicago. She was born 1826, and died
in Chicago in 1896, and was laid to rest at the side of
her husband in Mount Maarabh Cemetery. She remembered the congregation in her will, bequeathing to K.
A. M. a handsome sum of money. These two staunch
friends of K. A. M. will long be remembered in Chicago, and in the annals of the congregation their honored names are indelibly inscribed for everlasting
respect and gratitude.

The third President of K. A. M. was Abraham
Kohn. He was born in 1819, in Moenichsroth, Bavaria. He came to America with his brother Moses.
For a time they lived in New York, where they were
joined by a third brother, Judas, and the three brothers
then peddled in the State of Massachusetts. The section of the state in which they peddled was mostly
inhabited by Millerites, a religious sect founded by

William Miller of Massachusetts, holding peculiar
millenial views.   About 1843 the millenium was ex-
pected by as many as 50,000 believers in the doctrines
of Miller.   Business suffered very much in that section.
as the Millerites were preparing for the millenium and
bought nothing.   The three traveling merchants determined to go West.   They read in the papers that far
in the western country there was a promising town of the
name of Chicago, a good point where to start in business.   They bought a stock of dry goods and notions,
and went to Chicago.

Abraham Kohn became very popular in the Chicago
Jewish community.   He was a man of excellent quali-
ties.   He was a truly religious man, endowed with a
fine mind and administrative ability, which he cheer-
fully devoted to the service of his congregation.   He
received a very good education in his native town and
was quite a Hebrew scholar.   He was a diligent reader,
and quickly acquired knowledge of the English language. and was truly public spirited.   All this
fitted him admirably to be a leader among men.
The Chicago citizens recognized his superior abilities
and he was called to the office of City Clerk in 1861,
under Mayor John Wentworth.

He took an active part in arousing his American
co-religionists to protest against the Swiss treaty, which
excluded the Jewish citizens from the treaty rights
accorded to citizens of other faiths.   He was also an
enthusiastic advocate of the establishment of a rabbinical college in this country. and wrote several spirited
articles on the subject in the *American Israelite*.

The congregation needed just such a man, and the
members, highly appreciating his aptitude, followed his
leadership with the greatest confidence.   The congre-

REV. IGNATZ KUNREUTHER.

gation prospered to a high degree under his very able administration, and owes an everlasting debt of gratitude to this faithful and superior executive officer. Abraham Kohn was in office for three years, from 1853 to 1856. The order of service in the synagogue, which was well adapted to the needs of the members of the congregation during the first period of its existence, was arranged by him, and in later years, when the advancing spirit of the congregation demanded a change in the mode of worship, it was he again to whom the congregation looked for counsel and instruction. He died in Chicago in March, 1871, deeply mourned by the entire community.

In 1852 there arrived in Chicago a gifted young Jewish teacher from Germany by the name of Leopold Mayer, and Congregation Anshe Maarabh invited him to deliver a sermon in its synagogue. On the first day of Passover of that year, Mr. Leopold Mayer preached the first German sermon in the Jewish community of Chicago. In his sermon he made a strong plea for the introduction of the German language into the services of the synagogue, urging that the prayers of the ritual be recited in a living language. His address was well received, and the congregation honored him with a vote of thanks for his excellent effort. For a number of years Mr. Leopold Mayer gave religious instruction to the Jewish children of Chicago. He soon joined the congregation and became a popular leader in the community. He held the office of Secretary in K. A. M. for three years and was repeatedly elected trustee of the congregation. Mr. Mayer is living in our midst to-day, honored and respected by all. He is at present a Director of the Jewish Orphans Home of Chicago.

In 1853 the congregation established a day school where Hebrew was taught in addition to the common English branches. A number of non-Jewish teachers were engaged, among them Mr. Brewster and Mr. Gleason. who instructed with success in the K. A. M. school for many years. This day school was in operation for twenty years, until 1873, when it was discontinued and a Sabbath school, for religious instruction exclusively. was established in its stead.

The accompanying document, a certificate of the first confirmation and admission of a Quaker girl into the Jewish faith by a board of three rabbis in the city of Chicago, will no doubt be read with interest. Rev. Isidor Kalish came expressly from Cleveland, Ohio, to assist in the ceremony of conversion. He and Rev. Ignatz Kunreuther appointed Mr. Samuel Straus to act as the third of the rabbinical board. The lady in question was Mrs. C. F. Spiegel, relict of the brave Colonel M. Spiegel, who raised a company in Ohio to fight for the Union cause in the civil war. He entered the Union army as Captain. was soon raised for merit to the rank of Major, and by his bravery quickly rose to the rank of Colonel. He was about to be breveted General when he fell on the field of honor in the Red River expedition. May 4, 1864. Mrs. Spiegel is the mother of Mrs. Martin Barbe, a lady well known in the best Jewish circles of Chicago.

Colonel Spiegel moved to Chicago from Ohio. with his young bride, in 1853, and subsequently became identified with several of the local Jewish institutions. He was a prominent member of the Hebrew Benevolent Society and other organizations. Mrs. Spiegel is still living in Chicago.

In 1854 the congregation increased to such an

LEVI ROSENFELD.

CONVERSION CERTIFICATE.

Chicago, Cook County, Illinois, United States of America.

REV. RABBI KALISH,
REV. I. KUNREUTHER, *Constituted Rabinate Collegium.*
REV. SAMUEL STRAUS,

TO

HANNAH בת ABRAHAM, THE PATRIARCH.

CERTIFICATE OF CONVERTION

Know All Men by These Presents, that

Whereas, CAROLINE F. HAMLIN, from Lymaville, Stark County, in the State of Ohio, in the United States of America, personally appeared before us and declared: *That* from her own free will she desires to become a Jewess; *that* she has no earthly advantage nor fear in view, but *that* from inward persuasions of the high and sacred truths of Mosaism, she can find her perfect happiness only in the faith of Israel.

IN REFERENCE THERETO, we have caused an investigation into her principles and found her, according to our knowledge, conscience capable and worthy of convertion. And we hereby certify, that we have this day converted her to Judaism, according to Jewish rites, in the name of

חנה בת אברהם

In witness whereof we hereunto set our hands this 21st August, 5613 A. M., Chicago, Ill.

ISIDOR KALISH, [SEAL]
RABBI.
I. KUNREUTHER, [SEAL]
SAMUEL STRAUS, [SEAL]

extent that it became necessary to have a larger house
of worship, and K. A. M. purchased the northeast
corner of Adams and Wells streets, on which the building from Clark Street was moved, and a basement built
under it for a school and meeting rooms.

Samuel Straus, whose name appears on the certificate of conversion, in connection with the other two
rabbis, was elected a member of K. A. M. in 1854.   He
was often requested by the Board of Administration to
assist in reading the prayers, especially on New Year's
Day and Day of Atonement.

With the advance of the year 1855 an era of pros-
perity commenced for Congregation K. A. M.   In that
year a strong wave of new life seems to have rushed
into the Jewish community.   The congregation devel-
oped increased activity, its ranks were augmented by
considerable additions and the prospects became
brighter and brighter.   A new constitution was framed
and adopted.   The congregation was incorporated, a
special charter was obtained from the State of Illinois.

CHARTER OF CONGREGATION K. A. M., GRANTED BY THE LEGISLA-
TURE OF THE STATE OF ILLINOIS IN 1855.

AN ACT

TO INCORPORATE CERTAIN PERSONS THEREIN NAMED FOR RELI-
GIOUS PURPOSES.

SEC. I. *Be it enacted by the People of the State of Illinois, repre-
sented in the General Assembly,* That Abraham Kohn, Jacob Fuller,
Jacob Rosenberg, Joseph Liebenstein, Bernhard Sondheim, Lipp-
man Fish, and Abraham Rubel, and their successors in office, and
such other persons as are now, or hereafter may be, associated with
them for that purpose, are hereby constituted a body corporate, by
the name and style of

KEHILATH ANSHE MAYRIV,

in the City of Chicago, and by that name and style shall have per-
petual succession and a common seal.

ABRAHAM KOHN.

SEC. II. That said corporation shall have power to acquire land for the use of a synagogue, a parsonage, a school-house, and a burial place, and may erect all necessary buildings and enclosures thereon; may make and ordain such constitution, by-laws and regulations for their government, as they may deem necessary, not inconsistent with the Constitution and laws of this State or of the United States, and such constitution and by-laws shall be binding and obligatory upon all the members of said society or association, and may be enforced against them, provided that the value of the land acquired under the authority of this Act shall not exceed one hundred thousand dollars in the aggregate.

SEC. III. The said corporation shall also possess all the powers, and shall be subject to all the liabilities and restrictions and prescribed in Division Three, title, "Religious Societies," of Chapter Twenty-five of the Revised Statutes, which are not inconsistent with the provisions of this Act.

SEC. IV. That all engagements and obligations undertaken or assumed by the officers of said corporation, in conformity with the constitution, by-laws and regulations thereof, shall be binding and obligatory upon all the members of said corporation, who shall unite therewith by signing the constitution of said society or corporation, until such obligations or undertakings have been satisfied, and no person can withdraw therefrom until he shall have paid his assessments or dues as fixed by the constitution and by-laws and regulations of said society or corporation.

SEC. V. This Act shall take effect upon its passage, but may be altered, amended, or repealed by the Legislative Assembly.

THOS. S. TURNER,
Speaker of the House of Representatives.
G. KOERNER,
Speaker of the Senate.

Approved February 12, 1855.
J. A. MATTESON.

UNITED STATES OF AMERICA, ⎱
⎰ ss.
STATE OF ILLINOIS. ⎰

I, Alexander Starne, Secretary of State for the State of Illinois, do hereby certify that the foregoing is a true copy of an enrolled law now on file in my office.

In testimony whereof, I have hereunto set my hand and affixed the Seal of said State, this 12th day of February, A. D. 1855.

[SEAL]   ALEXANDER STARNE, *Secretary of State.*

In the same year a resolution was adopted to buy a new burial ground. A committee was appointed and instructed to select a piece of ground suitable for the purpose, and upon the recommendation of this committee in 1856 a parcel of ground in the town of Lake View, at the corner of Green Bay Road (now North Clark Street) and Belmont Avenue. containing about four acres, was bought for the sum of $2,400.00.   The old burial ground was indeed no longer fit for its purpose.   The fence. constantly exposed to the violent windstorms from Lake Michigan. had fallen to pieces, and the heaps of sand blowing in from the shore covered the graves and the marks of identification. The wall was rebuilt and the graves cleared from the accumulated heaps of sand, but the cemetery was soon again in the old dilapidated condition.   It was neither a suitable place for the dead nor a very inviting spot for the living.   It was abandoned on the 11th day of June, 1857. when the first interment took place in the new burial ground.

The number of interments in the old burial ground up to the time of its abandonment was about 150.

The new cemetery in Lake View was inclosed and laid out in family lots. The bodies from the first cemetery were removed to the new burial ground; the land was subsequently. in 1882, sold to the Lincoln Park Commissioners, and the first cemetery of the Jewish community of Chicago now forms a part of Lincoln Park.

The Jewish population of Chicago must have increased. indeed.   For a while one *bar mitzvah* follows the other. and the services on the Sabbath day are exceptionally well attended.   In November, 1854, Henry L. Frank was confirmed in K. A. M. syna-

SAMUEL COLE.

gogue. In the month of April Julius Mayer. now living in St. Joseph, Mo., was the first one to appear in the synagogue to be admitted into the fold of Judaism as a responsible member. He was followed on the succeeding Saturday by Martin Barbe. A week later David S. Greenebaum was confirmed, and he was followed by Leon Mandel.

In 1854 Rev. Isidor Lebrecht became teacher, reader and shochet of K. A. M.

Rev. Isidor Lebrecht was born January 11, 1805, in Niederstetten, Wurtemberg. He came to America September 3, 1854, and lived in New York for about six months, when he received a call from K. A. M. as cantor, teacher and shochet. His official connection with the congregation was of short duration, and he soon retired to private life. For many years he was a familiar figure in Jewish circles of Chicago.

In 1856 President Abraham Kohn resigned his office, and Samuel Cole was elected President for the unexpired term. The spiritual leader of the congregation at that time was Rev. G. M. Cohen. He remained only a short time with K. A. M., and then left for Cleveland. Samuel Cole was born in Yarotchin, Grand Duchy of Posen, Prussia, January 22, 1812. He came to America in 1837, and to Chicago in the year 1845. For many years he was a very active member of K. A. M., holding different offices of trust at various times in the congregation, and always filling them to the full satisfaction of his constituents.

The year 1857 marks the beginning of very important events in the life of Congregation Anshe Maarabh. The founders of the congregation were men of deeply rooted religious convictions, sound judgment and fixed opinions. They started the congregation on

a basis of rational conservatism, and to this they held
on with might and main. The flood of new ideas, with
which the rushing years deluged the advancing world,
did not pass over them unheeded. The powerful force
of progress moved them forward quite a distance in the
onward march of humanity. They could not resist the
mighty influences of the times. But, as men of prudence
and circumspection, they advanced slowly and cautiously,
always endeavoring to remain within the lines of conservatism, never losing sight of their main aim, their
cardinal principle and original intention, to perpetuate
Judaism, Jewish life and Jewish thought, and to leave it
to their children as they themselves inherited it from
their fathers. The effervescent spirits of the newer
members of the congregation considered this tenacious
tendency of cautious conservatism much too slow. They
wanted to ride on the wings of the whirlwind of reform,
to rush onward in the chariot race of the storm of
innovation, and the two elements of the congregation
could not amalgamate, they could not agree on a compromise. This was detrimental to peace and harmony.
The feeling of union was constantly disturbed, parties
formed themselves in the ranks of the members, and the
continued agitation retarded for a time the growth and
development of the congregation. "Reform" became
the slogan of the day with a number of the members of
the Chicago Jewish community. Dr. Einhorn's burning
eloquence, which he used with full force in the periodical
"Sinai," which he published at that time in Baltimore,
Md., set the souls of the Chicago enthusiasts on fire,
and "Light, more light!" was the cry on all sides.
At that time Dr. B. Felsenthal published his pamphlet
"Kol Kore Bammidbar" ("A voice calling in the
wilderness"), and his strong plea for reform aroused the

progressive element of the Chicago Jewish community
to feverish activity. A new congregation by the name
of " *Ohabe Or* " ("Lovers of Light") was formed, in
which the brothers Leon and Samuel Straus were the
leading spirits. They engaged a minister, a certain
Rev. Dr. Cohen, and instituted a temporary synagogue
in which they held public services. This congregation
existed only a few months, but it helped to influence the
members of K. A. M., who were now divided into two
camps, the conservative and the reform parties, to stand
in more determined antagonism against each other. The
"Ohabe Or" congregation was the precursor of the
"Reform Verein," which was established in June, 1858,
with Elias Greenebaum as President and Dr. Felsenthal
Secretary. This " Reform Verein" became the basis
upon which the "Sinai" congregation was built in 1861.

During this period of reform agitation, from 1857 to
1861, the ministrations of two men who held the office
of Rabbi in K. A. M. in succession promised to heal
the breach which was widening from day to day, but
neither of them was destined to accomplish this mission of peace and harmony. The first one was a certain Dr. M. Mensor, who started on his mission with a
loud blare of trumpets. Dr. Mensor hailed from Dublin,
Ireland. He came here well recommended, and the congregation placed its entire confidence in him, hoping to
reap the full benefit from the ministry of a pious,
honest and sincere teacher of Judaism. In fact. he
appeared to be all that. In the pulpit he stood wearing
a cap on the front of which were embroidered the
words, ליי׳ קדש ("Holy unto the Lord"), and the
lectures, which he delivered in fluent English, breathed
the spirit of piety and devotion to the cause of Israel.
But it was not long ere the deceived congregation

discovered the grave mistake which it had made in
electing this man Mensor as its spiritual guide, and
steps were taken to vacate the pulpit.

Dr. Mensor had been elected by the congregation in
October, 1857. In a general meeting held in February,
1858, the congregation passed a resolution requesting
Dr. Mensor to revise the ritual, and his proposed
revision was unanimously adopted. This was the first
and the last act of consequence which he accomplished
during his stay in Chicago. In November, 1858, he
was paid for nine months' salary in advance, given traveling expenses, and this German-Irish gentleman, with
his high-priest cap, his Hibernian wife and his plagiar-
ized stock of sermons, was sent back to the Emerald
Isle, and nothing more has ever been heard of him in a
Jewish pulpit.

In September, 1857, an election of officers was to
take place in the congregation, and for weeks previous
to this election the two factions were as busy as bees
with preparations for the coming battle. The 27th of
September arrived; both parties, the conservative faction, with Abraham Kohn as leader, and the reform
party, with Elias Greenebaum as marshal, mustered
their full forces. The election of President was the
contested point. The conservative party nominated
Samuel Cole, the temporary incumbent, and the candidate of the reform faction was Elias Greenebaum. The
last named gentleman was the regular nominee for
Vice-President, but at the eleventh hour he was nominated for President by the reform party. Before the
election took place a considerable amount of money
was paid in for such members as were in arrears with
their dues, in order to get their votes. The fight was
hard and bitter, for, in those days, the Jews took a

Rev. ISIDOR LEBRECHT.

warm interest in their religion and in the affairs of their religious institutions. Finally the reform party won the day by the election of its candidate. We quote the full result of this spirited election from the columns of the *American Israelite* of October 18, 1857:

President—Elias Greenebaum.

Vice-President—Ben. Schlossman.

Secretary and First Trustee—Leopold Mayer.

Second Trustee—Joseph Liebenstein.

Third Trustee—Bernhard Barbe.

Fourth Trustee—Jacob Benjamin.

Fifth Trustee—Henry Foreman.

The watchword of the conservative leader was "Peace, Harmony, and Moderate Reform."

"Equality, Reform and Education" was the motto of the successful candidate.

Elias Greenebaum, the fifth President of the K. A. M., was born in Eppelsheim, Rhenish Hessia, in the year 1822. He came to America in 1847, and a year later he settled in Chicago. He joined the congregation in 1850, was elected Secretary soon after, and held this office for three years. He was an officer of K. A. M. nearly all the time until 1860. President Greenebaum was the first one to agitate for a change in the ritual. He and his followers wished to have the prayer book of the Reform Temple in Hamburg, Germany, introduced in K. A. M., instead of the Roedelheimer Siddur, which was then in use.

Mr. Greenebaum is still a good and useful member of the Chicago community. At the age of 75 years he is as active as a man of 45, and to the joy of his honored wife and worthy children, as well as to the pride of this community at large, he gives promise of remaining in our midst for many years to come.

Simultaneously with Dr. Mayer Mensor, Congregation K. A. M. enjoyed the efficient services of Lipman Levi as reader and teacher in its school. Mr. Levi was born in Esslingen, Wurtemberg, December 19, 1813, and early evinced a taste for learning. Dissatisfied with the narrow curriculum which his birthplace offered, he continued his studies in a higher school in his native country. Later he became a teacher, and for twenty-three years instructed the young in Jebenhausen. He came to Chicago from New Haven in 1856, and was for some time reader and teacher in Congregation Anshe Maarabh. Even in his last years the thirst for knowledge did not leave him, and he spent the greater part of his time in reading. His kindly nature and mild, gentle manner endeared him to all who learned to know him, and when he died suddenly, Sunday, September 15, 1889, he left a host of friends to mourn his loss.

The congregation progressed again, the membership increased, the school was in good condition under Mr. Levi.

In the meetings of the Board and congregation an agitation for the introduction of an organ and a permanent choir for the services was carried on by the progressive faction, and caused many a spirited debate and many hard word-combats.

The second man whose appearance in the pulpit of K. A. M. promised to assuage the bitter feelings of antagonism developing between the different parties, and to re-establish peace, was Dr. Solomon Friedlander. From November, 1858, to 1860, the pulpit of K. A. M. was vacant, and the services were conducted by a Hazzan. Dr. Friedlander succeeded Dr. Mensor, who was a total failure as a peacemaker, in March, 1860, as teacher

ELIAS GREENEBAUM.

of Congregation Anshe Maarabh. He was a highly gifted and promising man of thirty-five years of age, who gained friends very fast. He was a fine rabbinical scholar and an excellent teacher, and he was soon requested to preach. His influence on the congregation would surely have been a very beneficial one. But, unfortunately for the highly agitated community, this good man died after having held the office of rabbi but a short time. He was bitten by a spider and soon blood-poison set in. He died on the 22d of August, six months after his arrival in Chicago. With the death of this man Congregation Anshe Maarabh was again disappointed, for the last hope of peace faded away, and it became evident that a split in the congregation must be the ultimate result of the growing feeling of dissatisfaction.

Dr. Solomon Friedlander was born on the 23d of October, 1825, at Brilon, Westphalia. He was the grandson of the venerable reform friend, Rabbi Joseph Abraham Friedlander, who gained fame in the controversy following the starting of the Hamburg Reform Temple in 1818. Dr. S. Friedlander entered the University of Bonn at a very early age, and later became a student at the University of Heidelberg, where he made theology and philosophy his special studies. He graduated as Doctor of Philosophy when he was only nineteen years of age, and his academic dissertation, which he wrote in his eighteenth year, called the attention of the world of letters to his great learning. In 1847 he was elected associate preacher to Dr. Holdheim, in the Berlin Reform Society, where he remained for one year. He was afterwards elected Professor in the Jewish Teacher's Seminary at Munster, and at the same time he preached in the Jewish Temple of that city.

In 1847 he began to publish in Leipzig a history of the Israelitish People, of which only three volumes were issued. In the same year appeared in print his "Sermons delivered in the Temple of the Jewish Reform Society at Berlin," and in 1850 he published at Brilon "The Life of the Prophets." He was not satisfied with his place in Munster, and returned to the University, where he studied medicine. He was soon awarded a diploma. But he was unsuccessful in practical life, and in 1855 he emigrated to America and landed in New York. Here, too, he was very unsuccessful in his medical practice, and he finally accepted the position of teacher in Congregation Anshe Maarabh of Chicago. His sad and sudden end in this city cast a veil of gloom on the Jewish community. His body was taken to Europe by his wife.

The majority of the members of K. A. M. were then ready to make some concessions to the minority. They were willing to retain the choir, to have the three-year cycle for the reading of the weekly portions of the Law during Sabbath services, and to do something substantial for the education of the Jewish children of Chicago.

At a meeting of the congregation held November 6th, 1859, a resolution was passed to pay $1.000 toward a Jewish public school, where the children of the Chicago Israelites should be instructed in the Hebrew and English languages and in religion. A committee consisting of nine members was appointed to carry out this plan.

On Saturday, May 28th, an organ, built by Mr. Wolfram of Chicago, was consecrated, and played for the first time in the synagogue. Mr. Molter was elected organist. Mrs. S. Alschuler sang the solo in Halevi's master composition, "*Min Hammetzar,*" and

LIPMAN LEVI.

the congregation was deeply impressed by the beautiful music.

The successor of Elias Greenebaum as President of the congregation was Benedict Schlossman, who assumed the duties of his office in 1859. He shared the reform ideas of his predecessor, but was more aggressive in his methods.

Mr. Schlossman was born in Steinhard, Bavaria, in 1816. He came to America in 1839 and settled in Eugene, Vermilion County, Indiana. He moved to Chicago in 1848.

The successor of Dr. Solomon Friedlander as teacher of the K. A. M. school was Rev. Marx Moses, formerly Hazzan of Lodge Street Synagogue in Cincinnati, Ohio, and then cantor of Attorney Street Synagogue *Shaare Rachamim* in New York. He was unanimously elected reader and requested to lead the choir. President Schlossman induced the trustees to consent to female singing in the synagogue, and a new choir was engaged, consisting of Misses Engel, S. Alschuler, M. Brunswick and H. Adler.

The congregation numbered 107 members or families, and was in every respect in a prosperous condition. President Schlossman and Rev. Moses did good service in their respective offices. Rev. Moses improved the mode of worship, and Schlossman kept up the spirit of activity and progress. The congregation decided to enlarge the synagogue and to re-dedicate it on the coming Passover feast.

In 1860 Dr. B. Felsenthal was invited by congregation K. A. M. to preach in its synagogue on the New Year's Day. The Doctor accepted and delivered a scholarly sermon on the significance of the shophar sounds. The address was highly appreciated by the congregation and was published under the title of " Schophar Klaenge."

The year 1861 will forever remain a memorable one in the annals of K. A. M. In that year Mr. M. M. Gerstley was elected President, and Rev. Dr. Liebman Adler was called from Detroit to the office of Rabbi and teacher. These two men, so well beloved and so highly respected, came to lead the congregation just in a time when their efficient services were most needed.

The question of ritual was still agitating the minds of the members. Resolutions were adopted in one meeting and reconsidered in another. Minhag Hamburg was proposed by one group and the Merzbacher Prayer-book by another. As a compromise Minhag Frankfort was re-introduced, but shortly afterwards again discarded. The reform party of the congregation was now restless and dissatisfied, and the conservative element unyielding and persistent. Towards the close of 1861 twenty-six members seceded from K. A. M. and formed a new organization under the name of " Sinai Congregation." Among the withdrawing members were some of the brightest and most liberal supporters of K. A. M., men like Henry Greenebaum. Elias Greenebaum, Leopold Mayer and others. But Congregation Anshe Maarabh stood the shock bravely. Peace now reigned in its midst, and under the guidance of President Gerstley and Rabbi Adler, K. A. M. started hopefully on the road to new triumphs. The membership kept on increasing so that the synagogue proved inadequate to accommodate the many worshipers.

In November, 1868, the congregation purchased the northwest corner of Wabash Avenue and Peck Court, with the church building standing upon it, for the sum of $50,000. The church was remodeled and changed

BENEDICT SCHLOSSMAN.

into a synagogue, and the congregation soon moved into the new edifice. The order of worship was again improved, a new organ, an excellent choir and other reforms were introduced, and the members were once more united and satisfied.

Mr. M. M. Gerstley, the eighth President of K. A. M., was born in the village of Fellheim, Bavaria, August 17, 1812. He received for those days a good education. In early youth he went to his brother in Vienna, Austria. There he became very much dissatisfied with the laws restricting the Jews, and in 1839 he came to America. After living for several years in Pennsylvania, chance led him to Chicago in 1848, and he made this city his home. He gave much of his time and attention to the various organizations with which he was connected. Soon after his arrival he joined Congregation K. A. M., in 1849. In 1856 he was Secretary of the congregation, and for a number of years he was Chairman of the School Board. For thirty years, from 1861 to 1891, he held the office of President, and his strict business methods, his great tact, prudence and integrity were of inestimable benefit to the congregation. He took a warm interest in charitable work, and was for some years Vice-President of the Hebrew Relief Association, and was actively identified with the work of that institution until old age and failing health forced him to retire. In 1891 he declined to be re-elected President of K. A. M. for the same reason.

Mr. Gerstley was an indefatigable worker, systematic and conscientious in all his transactions, kind and courteous in his intercourse with his fellow-men, commanding the greatest respect of all who came in contact with him. It was a perfect pleasure to have any dealings with him, for he was under all circumstances calm, collected and considerate. He was a student and a thinker, and his fertile brain was stored with a considerable amount of sound. practical knowledge—knowledge of human nature. He was of a religious turn of mind. well versed in the Bible and biblical literature, but he was no bigot, for he loved progress and was a warm friend of modern thought and teachings. The children of the K. A. M. Sabbath School and the older sons and daughters of the members of the congregation were always sure to find in him a faithful advocate and champion of their rights, and all therefore loved and honored him. He possessed the art of directing and correcting a subordinate without hurting his feelings. and by such means he gained unquestioned obedience for his orders. He talked to everybody like a friend, and the force of his logic never failed to convince.

After a long and useful life he was gathered unto his fathers Saturday, April 29, 1893.

During the thirty years in which he held the office of President in K. A. M., he delivered a number of addresses in the meetings of the congregation. Some of them were printed in pamphlet form. In an appendix the reader will find an address delivered by him at the dedication of the present temple, a short time before he resigned his office. This address was of great assistance to the writers of this history.

Rev. Liebman Adler was born on the 9th of January, 1812, at the town of Lengsfeld, in the Grand Duchy of Saxe-Weimar. His father, Judah Adler, was also a teacher. Until his thirteenth year he received instruction partly at his father's school and partly at a preparatory school in the vicinity, presided over by a clergyman. He also received Hebrew instruction from Rabbi Isaac Hess. then rabbi at Lengsfeld. His later studies

M. M. GERSTLEY.

in Talmud and Rabbinica he continued under Rev. Kunreuther, the father of Rev. Ignatz Kunreuther, who was
Rabbi at Gelnhausen, then at the Jewish high school,
in Frankfort-on-the-Main, under Rabbi Solomon Trier
and Rabbi Aaron Fuld, and later in the teachers' seminary at Weimar. After two years' study here he
graduated as teacher and was given charge of the Jewish
congregational school of his native town, Lengsfeld. In
1849 this school was united with the public school at
Lengsfeld, and Adler was appointed head teacher of the
amalgamated school. Liebman Adler was teacher by
choice, he loved his profession with all his heart and
with all his soul, and nature seemed to have selected
and endowed him especially for this profession. He
consequently was very successful in his work in the
school room.

In the year 1854 he left his native country and emigrated to America. A few months after his arrival in
this country he was elected preacher in the Detroit congregation, where he remained until the spring of 1861.
In that year he was called to Chicago by Kehillath
Anshe Maarabh, and here he preached and taught for
many years, and became a blessing to the whole community. His entire activity, all the rich treasures of
his great mind, his golden thoughts and his vast knowledge, he devoted to his congregation and to its school.
He held the light of truth aloft, and showed the leaders
and members of K. A. M., who became his warm admirers and faithful friends, the path of righteousness
and uprightness. A whole generation grew up to man-
hood and womanhood under his guiding love and instruction, and their hearts overflowed with affection,
gratitude and veneration for their true-hearted and
learned teacher until the name of Adler became a

household word in the entire Chicago community.
He possessed the gift of endurance and patience in a
very high degree, and was kind to every one. His
spirit overflowed with sparkling humor, yet he could be
earnest, and his words of wisdom made the deepest impression. He could win the most hardened heart with
his gentleness, and soothe the weeping soul with the
magic of his sympathetic utterances of consolation.

Liebman Adler was a warm patriot in the truest
sense of the word. During the years of doubt and sus-
pense, when the fate of the Union hung in the balance,
and the stoutest hearts failed and faltered, he flashed
rays of hope and enthusiasm into the hearts of his fel-
low-citizens. He raised his voice against shameful
slavery, and spoke most earnestly for the cause of union
and liberty. He inspired the souls of his congregation
from the pulpit with the justice of emancipation, and
sustained with hope the sympathies he aroused. A pamphlet containing five of his patriotic speeches, delivered
in the pulpit of K. A. M., was published in 1866, and
these speeches give evidence of his abhorrence of the
institution of slavery and his love of freedom. The
fact that he sent his oldest, at that time very young,
son to enlist in the Union army, to offer his life for the
preservation of the Union, is illustrious proof of the
sincerity of his utterances.

As a religious teacher and preacher he was consist-
ently conservative, clinging to old-time customs and
usages, but he never was an obscurant. His thoughts
were clear and free from bigotry; he fully understood
the demands of modern times, and was therefore toler-
ant to the opinions and claims of the young generation.
He gathered his inimitable sermons and published
them during the last years of his life in a work consist-

RIV. DR. LIEBMAN ADLER.

ing of two volumes, which he called צאינה וראינה, after the name of a well known religious book, which, during the last two centuries, had been very popular among the Jews of Germany and adjacent countries. The Press throughout the country paid him a just tribute of praise for this monumental work.

Rev. Adler was a frequent contributor to the Jewish journals of this country. He wrote many scholarly articles on a variety of subjects. It is especially the "*Deborah*" of Cincinnati, to which he was a steady contributor for many years, and in which some of his very best efforts were published.

On February 20, 1872, Rev. Adler was released by the congregation from preaching, and elected as teacher and reader. This was done in order to enable the congregation to engage an English-speaking minister, as Rev. Adler preached mostly in the German language. In the following month of March, Dr. M. Machol of Leavenworth, Kansas, was elected minister, and he occupied the pulpit of K. A. M. until 1876, and when he resigned Rev. Adler was again elected minister, reader and teacher, which position he held until 1883.

At a meeting of the congregation held November 5, 1882, the following resolution was unanimously carried:

WHEREAS, This congregation, fully recognizing the long and faithful services performed by its honored and much esteemed minister, Rev. Liebman Adler; be it, therefore,

Resolved, That this congregation, in meeting assembled, hereby pensions said Rev. Liebman Adler during the balance of his life.

On the 15th of January, 1882, Dr. Adler was 70 years of age, and the congregation celebrated his seventieth birthday in a befitting manner.

On the 29th of January, 1892, Rev. Liebman Adler, at the high age of 80 years, closed forever his peaceful

and blessed career on earth, to abide with the immortals
in the realms of bliss. As he lived so he died, patiently
enduring the pangs of a painful illness, thinking more
of others than of himself and uttering with his last
breath words of submission to the will of God, and
sentiments of love and admonition to his beloved wife
and dear children.

During the week preceding his demise and at a time
when he was intensely suffering from very acute pains.
Rev. Dr. Liebman Adler wrote a paper which he headed
"Mein letzter Wille" (My last Will). The document
is a brief one, and yet rich in its contents. On reading
his plain but touching words one cannot help being
deeply impressed with the outpouring of a grand soul
and of a truly pious heart. We deem it proper to
publish a *fac-simile* of it in the appendix. It charac-
terizes the man; it mirrors clearly his inner life; it
reflects his ideas and sentiments. It is so simple and
yet so sublime in its simplicity. It is the magic melody
of a dying Paganini, flooding the soul with joy and
the eyes with tears. It is a work created by a master
favored with rare inspiration, an idealized reality, an
ideal realized.

Our forefathers in former times used to call such a
document צַוָּאָה (Tzava'ah). modern writers name it
"Last Will" or "Ethical Testament." Truly. Liebman Adler's Last Will is such an "ethical Testament,"
which deserves to be printed here.—as a mark of honor
to the venerated Teacher, as a grateful remembrance of
the departed Rabbi and as an inspiring word for us
who are still among the living.

Adler and Gerstley! The death of these two
illustrious and faithful friends, leaders and benefactors
of K. A. M., closes an epoch in the history of the con-

gregation. To K. A. M. Gerstley and Adler are not dead. To it they are not mere shadows that flitted around for a while and then floated away into the darkness of death to be heeded no longer. To K. A. M. they are brilliant rays of light that will forever shine on its path to lead it onward and upward to God's truth and Israel's duty.

THE PRESENT.

AFTER THE GREAT FIRE.

N the 9th day of October, 1871, an ocean of fire swept over the Garden City. Churches, synagogues, private dwellings and public buildings were laid in ashes. Innumerable documents, the most valuable public records and registers of private possession were buried in the smoking ruins, consumed by the unchained element and irretrievably lost. Fortunately the Temple of K. A. M., corner Peck Court and Wabash Avenue, was untouched by the all-consuming conflagration. But all its books and documents were irrecoverably gone. The officers of the congregation for 1871–1872 were: President, M. M. Gerstley; Vice-President, Jacob Rosenberg; Treasurer, H. A. Kohn; Secretary, Joseph Pollack. The rest of the Board of Administration consisted of: Henry Steiner, Samuel Cole, S. Schlesinger, Emanuel Brunswick, B. Bruneman, Henry Hyman, Henry S. Haas, L. F. Leopold, Max Weineman and S. Straus. To the indomitable energy, liberality, circumspection and strict business tact of these men it is due that the congregation escaped with little loss. Joseph Pollack, the able Secretary of the congregation, was at that time clerk of Cook County; he had all the papers, books and records

belonging to the congregation in a vault in the Court
House, and there they were burned with all the registers and deeds of the county.   The books, which were
in the hands of the treasurer, H. A. Kohn, were also
consumed by the great fire, and the congregation found
itself without any proof of outstanding indebtedness to
be collected. even without a pew register indicating
the ownership of seats in the Temple.   In spite of
these, as it seemed. unsurmountable obstacles. order
was soon restored without hardly an interruption in the
regular run of the congregation's affairs.   In this connection we cannot refrain from mentioning the name of
a tried and trusty servant of K. A. M., who was em-
ployed for many years as sexton and collector.   The
name of this man was Marks Jackson.   He was born
in Galautch, in the Province of Posen. Prussia, February, 1819, came to Chicago, November. 1855, entered
the service of the congregation in the year 1857, and
remained in active usefulness until the end of 1893,
when he was generously pensioned.   He died in Chicago, October 28, 1894, aged 75 years.   His intelligence, efficiency and integrity were of great help to the
congregation, especially in those days of confusion
which followed the fire of 1871.   At a general meeting
held October 29, 1871, the second meeting after the
fire, the members showed their readiness to stand by the
congregation, to aid and to assist with might and main
to bring it back to the usual standard of financial pros-
perity. Mr. Jacob Rosenberg, the venerable Vice-
President, with his usual liberality, refused to accept
interest due him on a loan which he had advanced to
the congregation ; even Collector Jackson, in a letter
addressed to the Board of Administration, requested to
have $200 deducted from the annual salary voted to

Rev. Dr. M MACHOL.

him at his last election. Of course this was declined, with thanks, but it indicates the spirit prevailing at that time among all those who were connected with K. A. M.

On November 23, 1871, the use of the school rooms was granted to Sinai Congregation, whose Temple was destroyed by the fire.

In a meeting of the Board of Administration, November 26, President Gerstley read a letter from the trustees of the Universalist Society (Dr. Ryder, minister) asking for the use of the synagogue for religious service on Sunday mornings. This request was also granted.

The question of a change in the ritual now became the main topic for discussion. At a meeting of the Board, December 18th, on motion of Samuel Cole, it was resolved to recommend the adoption of Dr. Einhorn's prayer-book in the English translation. At a meeting of the congregation on January 9, 1872, this was complied with, but action was postponed.

On March 21, 1872, Dr. M. Machol of Leavenworth, Kansas, was unanimously elected minister of the congregation, to take the place of Adler, who was released from preaching.

Dr. M. Machol was born November 13, 1845, in Kolmar, Prussia. He received his theological education in the Seminary of Breslau, where he graduated as Rabbi in 1868. In February, 1869, he took charge of the pulpit of the congregation in Leavenworth, Kansas. He was Rabbi of K. A. M. for four years, from 1872 to 1876, when he accepted a call from Anshe Chesed Congregation of Cleveland, Ohio. For nearly twenty-two years he has preached to his Cleveland congregation, where he is much honored and beloved.

On April 4, 1872, it was resolved that the congregation again open a Day School. This school was discontinued in April, 1875, for want of scholars. School was held in a house on Thirteenth Street, between Wabash and Michigan Avenues, belonging to Lazarus Silverman.

The Merzbacher prayer-book was adopted in January, 1873, and the same is still in use to-day.

A motion to have Friday evening services, with choir and sermon, was also adopted at the same meeting.

The congregation joined the Union of American Hebrew Congregation, January 4, 1874.

In the second Chicago fire of July 1874, the congregation lost its synagogue, on corner Peck Court and Wabash Avenue, and was now homeless. The trustees of the Methodist Episcopal Church, on corner Wabash Avenue and Fourteenth Street, generously granted the use of their church to K. A. M., and regular Sabbath services were held there until the congregation had a house of worship of its own. In December, 1874, the congregation purchased the lot and church building from Plymouth Church, on the southeast corner of Indiana Avenue and Twenty-sixth Street, and changed it into a synagogue. This property, with all furniture, carpets, etc., was purchased by Nathan Eisendrath for K. A. M. for $20,000. Mr. Eisendrath's acquaintance with real estate values in that neighborhood, his prompt action and clear calculation saved the congregation quite a sum of money, for which a vote of thanks was tendered to him in meeting assembled on December 16, 1874. The lot on the corner of Peck Court and Wabash Avenue was sold for $32,000.

The synagogue, corner Twenty-sixth Street and Indiana Avenue, was dedicated on Friday, February 5,

FORMER K. A. M. TEMPLE,
S. E. COR. INDIANA AVENUE AND TWENTY-SIXTH STREET.

1875. Drs. Kohler, Felsenthal and Messing were invited to assist. The congregation then had a membership of 120, owned the property, corner Indiana Avenue and Twenty-sixth Street, was free from debt and had a nice surplus in the treasury. About 120 children attended the Sabbath school.

On a number of Sabbaths during the year 1883. Rev. Dr. E. G. Hirsch, minister of Sinai Congregation, delivered a series of sermons in the K. A. M. Temple, and at a meeting held August 20th, the Board expressed in a set of resolutions the congregation's appreciation of the Doctor's able efforts, and voted a substantial acknowledgment of his services.

On Kol Nidre Eve of the same year, the practice of collecting in the synagogue contributions for the support of the United Hebrew Charities was, for the first time, introduced.

In a meeting of the congregation, held September 9th, Henry N. Hart moved that the gentleman remove their hats during worship, and his motion was adopted by a good majority.

Dr. Samuel Sale of Har Sinai Congregation, Baltimore, Md., was elected minister of the congregation, August 5, 1883. He assumed charge of the pulpit during the following month of September. His able discourses made the most favorable impression. He remained with the congregation for four years. He was then tendered a re-election, which he declined, and accepted a call from Shaare Emeth Congregation of St. Louis, one of the largest and most influential congregations west of the Mississippi.

Dr. Sale was born October 29, 1854, in the city of Louisville. It was here that he received his earlier education, and his talents so manifested themselves already, at this early age, that at his graduation from the high school he was the valedictorian of his class, and received the distinction of a scholarship to Washington and Lee University of Lexington, Va. In September, 1873, he went to Europe, where, in October of the same year, he matriculated at the University of Berlin, and entered also the Hochschule fuer die Wissenschaft des Judenthums. Returning to his native land, after five years of study at these institutions with his degrees as Rabbi and Doctor, he received an immediate call to the pulpit of Har Sinai Congregation in Baltimore, made famous by the illustrious David Einhorn. With Har Sinai, Dr. Sale remained as Rabbi from Rosh Hashana, 1878, until September, 1883, when he came to Chicago to accept a call as successor to Dr. Adler. The four years of his ministry in Kehillath Anshe Maarabh deeply attached to him the hearts of all its members, and in the community of Chicago generally Dr. Sale won in this brief period a host of admirers and enthusiastic friends. In 1887, however, he had the choice of two calls. The one was from the Reform Congregation of Kenesth Israel of Philadelphia, one of the largest and most prosperous congregations in America; the other was from his present charge, Shaare Emeth of St. Louis. The residence in St. Louis of all the members of his paternal household made him look favorably upon the latter offer.

On June 10, 1896, he opened with prayer the Republican National Convention in St. Louis, at which McKinley was nominated for the Presidency.

Financially the congregation was then in an excellent condition; it received more revenue in that year than in any previous one.

In the month of April, 1888, Rabbi Isaac S. Moses

REV. DR. SAMUEL SALE.

of Nashville, Tenn., was elected minister of the congregation, and occupied the pulpit of K. A. M. for eight years.

Rabbi Moses was born fifty years ago in Santa Michael in the Province of Posen, Prussia, where his father was Rabbi. After graduating from the public school of his native town, he was sent to Gleiwitz. in Silesia. to the Real-gymnasium. From 1865 to 1869 he attended the Rabbinical Seminary at Breslau. In the year of 1872, he followed his oldest brother to America. His first position as Rabbi was in Quincy. Ill., where he remained for five years; he then was called to Milwaukee, Wis., and there he occupied the pulpit for eight years. During this period he published a German semi-monthly called "*Der Zeitgeist*," a paper which was very able conducted. For a brief period of nine months he was the Rabbi of the congregation at Nashville, Tenn., and then he accepted a call as minister from Congregation Anshe Maarabh. which he held from 1888 to 1896.

For several reasons he declined a re-election, and in September, 1896. he organized a People's Synagogue in the city, on the basis of minimum contributions. thus creating for himself an independent pulpit.

The town of Lake View, in which the cemetery of the congregation was located, had in the meantime increased its population, and built up its territory to such an extent, that the cemetery was now in the midst of a densely inhabited neighborhood. The people living in the houses adjacent to the burial ground looked down from their windows upon the graves. The neighbors as well as the congregation found this state of affairs to be annoying and unpleasant. The congregation decided to look out for a new place for a cemetery, and a committee was appointed to find suitable grounds. At a special meeting of the congregation, held June 3, 1888, the committee reported through its chairman, that, after investigating a number of offers, it had decided to recommend to the congregation the purchase of a tract of land in the town of Jefferson, containing twenty acres. The recommendation of the committee was concured in, and a motion carried, to empower the trustees to obtain a loan of $10,000 for the purchase of the land.

The venerable chairman of the Committee on Burial Ground, Mr. Jacob Rosenberg, the Vice-President and Patriarch of K. A. M., came forward with his wonted generosity and offered to loan it the sum of ten thousand dollars, without interest, for the purchase. At a special meeting of the congregation held July 16, 1888, Mr. Jacob Rosenberg made a new and more liberal proposition to the congregation. He offered to donate to K. A. M. the entire twenty acres for burial-ground purposes, and his generous offer was gratefully accepted. The ground was properly inclosed, and laid out in family lots. The Lake View cemetery was abandoned and the property subsequently sold.

The old cemetery was closed on the 27th of October, 1889, when the first interment in the new burial ground at Dunning Station, in the town of Jefferson, took place. 941 bodies were transferred from the old to the new cemetery, and 98 bodies were removed by parties to outside cemeteries.

Mr. Jacob Rosenberg, has by his unflagging care for the welfare of the congregation, won for himself the warmest appreciation of every member, for he stood at its cradle and with parental solicitude he helped to care for the infant congregation through all the fifty years of its development.

REV. DR. I. S. MOSES.

He was one of the fourteen who, in 1847, signed the first constitution of Kehillath Anshe Maarabh, and for forty-nine years he was an able and faithful officer of the congregation. He is the only surviving charter member of K. A. M., and has fully earned the place of honor which K. A. M. willingly and readily accords him on this occasion of its semi-centennial celebration.

Mr. Jacob Rosenberg was born at Altenmuhr, Bavaria, March 25, 1819. He came to America in 1837. He was eighteen years old when he arrived in New York. For four years he traded through New England and New York State, parts of Pennsylvania, Ohio and Indiana. In 1841 he came to Chicago. Here he found Levi Rosenfeld, and with him formed a copartnership under the firm name of Rosenfeld & Rosenberg. They were very successful, and in 1845, they were recognized as the most prosperous retail and wholesale dry goods merchants in the West. Mr. Rosenfeld had married a sister of Michael Reese. Another sister, Miss Hannah Reese, came to Chicago to visit Mrs. Rosenfeld, and in 1849, she became Mrs. Rosenberg. Theirs was the first Jewish wedding ever known in Chicago. For ten years Jacob Rosenberg was a volunteer fireman, member of Company I, or the Fire King. In 1876, he was selected by the municipal reformers of that year to stand in the second ward for alderman. He was elected by a handsome majority and served for two years with credit. He was auditor of the Chicago Industrial Exposition for several consecutive years. By the will of his brother-in-law, Michael Reese of San Francisco, $200,000 were given in trust to Mr. Rosenberg and Mrs. Rosenfeld, jointly, for benevolent objects in Chicago. They determined

to build and endow a hospital, to be called Michael
Reese Hospital. This they accomplished, and it is
now very justly a pride of the Jewish population of the
city. Mr. Rosenberg has been director of the United
Hebrew Charities since its inception. He is a truly
charitable man, giving systematically in proportion to
the merits of the various charities. His wife, who was
a true mother in Israel, was born in 1824, and died in
Chicago, January 16, 1890. With her good husband
she vied in devotion to K. A. M., and like her noble
sister, Mrs. Rosenfeld, she did not forget her congregation in her will, and K. A. M. holds her honored name
in grateful remembrance.

As the holidays of 1889 were approaching, it was
found by the Board of Administration that the auditorium of the synagogue was too small to comfortably
seat the members, and it was decided to obtain tem-
porarily larger quarters. The Immanuel Baptist
Church, on Michigan Avenue and Twenty-third Street,
was procured for use during the holidays, and the
cordial treatment accorded to K. A. M., by the officers
and pastor of the church, was gratefully acknowledged
by the congregation.

On December 5, 1889, the southeast corner of
Thirty-third Street and Indiana Avenue, with a frontage
of 120 feet on Indiana Avenue, was bought for the sum
of $36,000, and the present Temple was erected
thereon, furnished and equipped at a cost of $110,000.
The synagogue, on corner Twenty-sixth Street and
Indiana Avenue, was sold to Congregation Bnai Shalom
on March 16, 1890.

The new Temple was planned and erected under the
supervision of Messrs. Adler & Sullivan, the well-known
architects. It has 190 pews in the auditorium, 90 pews

K. A. M. TEMPLE,
INDIANA AVENUE AND THIRTY-THIRD STREET.

in the gallery, and a seating capacity of about 1,500 persons.

Mr. Dankmar Adler, the senior partner of the firm of architects named above, is the son of the late Rev. Dr. Liebman Adler, who, in the late Civil War, went to the front to serve the Union cause as a soldier. He is an honored member of K. A. M.

While the Temple was in course of building Sinai Congregation kindly offered its Temple to K. A. M. for Saturday services and Sunday School use. The generous offer was gratefully accepted.

According to the annual report of the President, submitted in 1890, the congregation had a membership of 155, and 30 widow members, a total of 185.

The new Temple was dedicated June 11, 1891, and Drs. Adler, Felsenthal, Hirsch, Stolz, Austrian, Messing and Norden, assisted Dr. Moses in the dedicatory ceremonies.

The congregation then had a total membership of 194.

On September 6, 1891, Mr. Henry N. Hart, the present incumbent, was unanimously elected President of K. A. M. Mr. Hart had always taken such a lively interest in the work of the congregation that no step of importance was undertaken for years without his wise and wakeful co-operation. In fact, many of the most beneficial measures which the congregation has passed during the last twenty years were instigated by Mr. Hart. While he zealously watched with his fellow members over the conservation of the congregation; while he earnestly sought with them to retain the true Jewish spirit in the midst of K. A. M., he at the same time endeavored to place his beloved congregation within reach of the shining rays of modern life,

of progressive decorum and decorous progress. Truly
the mantle of Gerstley, had fallen on a worthy Elisha!

Henry N. Hart, the eighth President of K. A. M.,
who for the last six years has been administering the
affairs of the congregation, was born in Eppelsheim,
Rhenish Hessia, in 1838. He came to America in 1854
with his elder brother, Abraham, and they settled in
Chicago. Twenty-seven years ago he joined K. A. M.
Since a number of years he has been a member of the
Board of Directors of the United Hebrew Charities,
and chairman of the Michael Reese Hospital Committee. He is also a director of the Humane Society,
and devotes much of his valuable time to charitable
work.

President Hart is assisted in the management of the
affairs of the congregation by four officers and ten
directors, who, with the President, constitute the Board
of Administration. The present officers are: Jacob
Rosenberg, Vice-President; Henry Gerstley, Treasurer;
Israel Cowen, Recording Secretary, and Jacob Newman,
Jr., Financial Secretary. The Directors are: Joseph
M. Schnadig, David Wormser, J. N. Strauss, Samuel
Spitz, L. H. Freiberger, Louis Benjamin, Sig. Silber-
man, Geo. Schlesinger, Simon H. Kohn and A. H.
Kohn.

In April, 1896, Mr. A. Sinks, who was teacher of
the K. A. M. Sabbath School for over twenty years,
was pensioned, with full salary, for life, and the Board
passed complimentary resolutions in praise of his long
and efficient services. Mr. Sinks has recently removed
to New York.

In the beginning of the current year Rev. M. P.
Jacobson, of Youngstown, Ohio, was elected to fill the
vacant pulpit of K. A. M., and during the short time

HENRY N. HART.

JACOB ROSENBERG, Vice-Pres.

HENRY GERSTLEY, Treas.

HENRY M. HART, President

ISRAEL COWEN, Sec'y.

J. NEWMAN JR., Fin. Sec't.

OFFICERS OF K. A. M., 1897.

L. H. FREIBERGER.   3 SAMUEL SPITZ.   8 GEO. SCHLESINGER.   7 DAVID WORMSER.
SIG. SILBERMAN   4 JOSEPH M. SCHNAIDIG.   9 LOUIS BENJAMIN.   8 A. H. KOHN
9 J. N. STRAUSS.   10 SIMON H. KOHN.

of his sojourn in the midst of the congregation, the new, young and scholarly Rabbi has gained a host of warm friends.

Rabbi Moses Perez Jacobson is a native of Ft. Wayne, Ind., where he was born August 25, 1864. At the age of seven he was placed in the Jewish Orphan Asylum in Cleveland, Ohio. It was here that he manifested his inclination for the Jewish ministry, being the recipient in every competitive examination of all the prizes given for Jewish studies. He is the holder also of the Simon Wolf Gold Medal of 1877, for natural philosophy. In 1878, he left Cleveland to enter the Hebrew Union College in Cincinnati. For the first four years of his college course he attended simultaneously "Hughes High School," from which, when he was graduated in 1882, he was honored with the Ray Silver Medal for the highest percentage in all studies during the entire four years. That same year the Hebrew Union College conferred upon him the degree of B. H. (Bachelor of Hebrew.)

Still continuing at the college, he pursued his secular studies at the University of Cincinnati, then known as the McMicken University. From both College and University, he was graduated in June, 1886, receiving from the latter his degree of B. A. (Bachelor of Arts), and from the former his ordination as rabbi. As early as January of this year he had been elected to the ministry of the Congregation Beth Israel of Macon, Ga., but did not enter upon his duties until September after his nomination. After three years of steady and earnest work here, he accepted a call to the Congregation Beth El of San Antonio, Texas. In 1891 a telegram from Salt Lake City, Utah, offering him the ministry of the newly built temple of Congregation

Bnai Israel, surprised him the very day when his San Antonio congregation had extended him a flattering tender of re-election. Climatic considerations induced him to decide in favor of Salt Lake City. In 1895 he determined to come East and took charge of the pulpit of Congregation Rodef Shalom of Youngstown, Ohio. The two years spent in this little city have been the warmest and the happiest possible to any ministerial experience, and the relation between Rabbi Jacobson and his members, one and all, was of the very most cordial nature; still, when in December, 1896, Rabbi Jacobson was invited to address Kehillath Anshe Maarabh on Saturday and Sunday, the 26th and 27th, he readily accepted. The impression made at that time led ultimately to his election here, dating from March 1, 1897. Rabbi Jacobson entered upon his office formally by his inaugural address, March 20.

During the absence of a minister, from July, 1896, to March, 1897, H. Eliassof, for many years teacher in the K. A. M. Sabbath School and now principal of the same, officiated as reader. The Sabbath School of K. A. M. has a staff of five teachers besides Mr. Eliassof, the Misses Irma Rosenthal, Ella Schottenfels, Flora Dryfuss, Leah Levy and Mr. Sam. Gerstley. The last named has volunteered his services. Rev. Jacobson is the superintendent of the school.

The congregation has at present a membership of 186, and about 200 children are enrolled as pupils of the Sabbath School.

Congregation K. A. M. is in a very prosperous condition. It owns a magnificent Temple and a valuable burial ground free from all incumbrance.

REV. DR. M. P. JACOBSON.

CONCLUSION.

In the midst of the harmonious sounds of melodious
music, the felicitations of friends, the joy and festivity
which this day of its golden jubilee brings to Congregation Anshe Maarabh, it stops for a brief moment to
cast a retrospective glance upon the past period of its
existence. The light of satisfaction illumines K. A.
M.'s countenance. From the distant past the star of
hope radiates its effulgence into the present. All the
trials and hardships which K. A. M. had to endure, to
conquer and to overcome, were not in vain! It has
reached a high aim in triumph, and it may hope to rise
still higher in the future. The grains planted by a
handful of Jewish pioneers and pathfinders fifty years
ago, had taken root, had sprouted, budded, bloomed,
ripened into fruit, and K. A. M. now reaps the golden
harvest. What has Congregation Anshe Maarabh
achieved during all these past fifty years? Has it
drifted on the sea of life aimlessly, without a compass
to point the right direction? Has it really retrogressed
to a standpoint of disharmony with the spirit of modern
Judaism and the tendencies of these times of progress?
No! K. A. M. has, to-day, the satisfaction of finding
itself in the front rank of the true friends of Judaism
as well as abreast of the age, on the road to a broader
humanity. Judaism was and still is the guiding star
on its course. If Congregation K. A. M. has done
nothing more in the past half a century of Jewish
congregational life in America than to preserve for the
younger generation of to-day the principle of an intel-

lectual fidelity to Judaism, this in itself should be
ample ground for joy and congratulation. In this con-
sciousness of being a true standard bearer of Israel's
message unto the world, it can be content to continue
on its way, trusting its future to the protection of Him
who has been the guardian of Israel through the ages,—
to the love and care of God.   And now *en avant!*

APPENDIX.

APPENDIX.

—

A LEAF FROM THE CONSTITUTION OF 1855.

— —

CONSTITUTION

OF

KEHILATII ANSHE MAYRIV.

————

PREAMBLE.

WE, the undersigned, members of the Religious Congregation of the Israelites of the city of Chicago, founded
on the third day of October, 5607, A. M., by fifteen members, do hereby adopt, and agree to obey, the following
Constitution, and the several By-Laws that may be enacted
in accordance with its provisions.

ARTICLE I.

Name of Congregation.

The name of this Congregation shall be

קהלת אנשי מערב

KEHILATH ANSHE MAYRIV.

ARTICLE II.

Officers of Congregation.

The affairs of the Congregation shall be managed by
ONE PRESIDENT, ONE VICE-PRESIDENT, FIVE TRUSTEES, and
ONE SECRETARY, subject to the provisions hereinafter con-
tained.

ARTICLE III.

Election of Officers.

1. The officers of this Congregation shall be elected by
ballot, at a meeting to be held annually on the first Sunday

Mein letzter Wille.

Ich wünsche, daß man sich mit meiner Beerdigung nicht beeile. Man soll nicht schon früher Leichenflecken einstellen, die Beerdigung nicht vor 48 Stunden nach meinem Verscheiden vornehmen zu lassen.

Sollte der mich zu behandelnde Arzt im Interesse der Wissenschaft eine Obduktion für wünschenswert halten, so möchte ich, daß man ihm die Vornahme einer solchen gestatte.

Mein Sarg soll nicht über 7 ℳ kosten.
Keine Blumen
Meine Leichenzug unmittelbar vom Sterbehause aus nach dem Lager überschließt.
Keine Leichenrede.

Liebe Henni! In Rücksicht auf Deine delikate Natur, wünsche ich, daß Du zu Hause bliebest u. nicht dem Leichenzuge folgest bis z. äußersten Hinausschen

Meine!

Nicht über drei Tage Trauer in häuslicher
Zurückgezogenheit.

Ich schätze das Kostliche meiner Söhne und der
Töchter nach Gebühr; aber nur, wenn ihr euch
nach Ablauf der Trauer erst nicht ebenso schätzt,
werde ich die Vorgezogenheit versäumen.

Nun Vermögensverhältnisse ab und ein
bau, sollte jedes meiner verheiratheten Kinder einer beliebigen und nach Gemeinde sich an-
schließen, am liebsten dem K. A. M.

Die nicht zu entfernt wohnenden Kinder
sollen sich die günstigsten Wohnorte u. und ab
ohne Störung das eigenen häuslichen Ver-
hältnisse geschehen und, jeden Freiberg und
und die Wohnung freuen.

Meine Kinder! Haltet als Geschwister
zusammen. Lasst euch dabei eine Ehre
zu schwer sein, euch einander beizustehen

u. geschwisterliche Gefühle zu pflegen.
Jede Liebesthat, die Ihr Euch einander
erzeiget, würde meiner Seele wohl
thun. Das Beispiel von H in Liebe u.
Treue zusammen haltender Kinder, nach Verlust
würde dem Grabe dieselbe ein schö-
nerer Schmuck sein als der prächtig
ste Blumenflor, auch den ich gern will,
gestern doch Eurem Belieben überlassen
bleibt.

Das bischen verzehrbares Vermögen
das ich hinterlasse, wird Euch erst nach
dem Tode der Mutter zu Gute kommen.
Ich kenne Euch; ich darf vertrauen, daß
ihr von Keinem von Euch über Besitz
u. Verwenung unkindlich begegnet wer-
den werde. Die Ehrschaft, die Ihr aber schon
besitzet, ist ein guter Name u. eine Er-
ziehung, so gut ich sie geben konnte. Es scheint
mir, als wäre Einer von Euch zum Reicheren
der vorgeholt sei. Laßt Euch das nicht den
Letzten. Bleibt nur stark schlicht, wahre,

glücklich u. zufrieden. Beneidet nicht! Es ist
keine Sache dabei, selbst wenn es gelückt.
Legt dann ganze Energie in die Führung
Eures Geschäfts. Kennt Gott
u. habt Ihn immer vor Augen, gegen
Menschen seid liebreich, zuvorkommend u.
bescheiden u. es wird Euch wohl gehen
euch ohne Reichthum

   Mein letztes Wort an Euch ist: Ehret
Eure Mutter! Erleichtert ihr den letzten
Weg Wittwenstand. Lasset ihr den Genuß
des kleinen Nachlasses ungestört u. hel-
fet nach, wo es fehlen sollte..
   Lebt wohl, Söhne u. Kinder!

Noch eins, Kinder. Ich weiß wohl, Ihr könnt
nicht, wie Ihr euch wolltet, Euer Judenthum
nach über noch neuer Auffassung u. wie
ich es geübt. Bleibet aber Juden u. lebt
als Juden in der besten Weise Eurer Zeit.
Nicht bloß für Euch sondern auch wo es
gilt, das Ganze zu fördern.

REV. DR. LIEBMAN ADLER'S LAST LETTER TO HIS FAMILY.

MY LAST WILL.

- -

I desire that there be no haste in my interment. If there are no signs of decomposition sooner, the funeral should not be until forty-eight hours after my death.

If the physician who treated me should find it desirable in the interest of science to hold a post-mortem examination, I would like that he be not interfered with.

My coffin shall not cost more than $7.

No flowers.

My funeral to be directly from the place of demise to the cemetery.

No funeral oration.

Dear Hannah : In view of your delicate health, I desire that you remain at home and not join the funeral if the weather is the least inclement.

Not more than three days' mourning in domestic retirement.

I cherish the kaddisch—prayers of mourning in the synagogue —of my sons and daughters as it deserves, but I do so only if you, after the expiration of the year of mourning, do not omit attendance at the synagogue without necessity.

If financial conditions permit, each of my married children should join a Jewish congregation, the fittest being the K. A. M.— Kehillath Anshe Maarabh, " Congregation of the Men of the West," corner of Indiana Avenue and Thirty-third Street.

Those children who do not live too distant should, if the weather permit, and if it can be done without disturbing their own domestic relations, gather every Friday evening around the mother.

My children, hold together. In this let no sacrifice be too great to assist each other and to uphold brotherly and sisterly sentiment. Each deed of love you do to one another would be balm to my soul. The example of eleven children of one father who stand together in love and trust would be to his grave a better decoration than the most magnificent wreath of flowers, which I willingly decline, but leave to your judgment.

The small savings which I leave will come to you only after the death of the mother. I know you; I may trust that you will not meet in an unfilial way about possession and disposition. The heritage which is already yours is a good name and as good an education as I could afford to give. It does not look as if any one of you had a disposition to grow rich. Do not be worried by it. Remain strictly honest, truthful, industrious and frugal. Do not speculate. No blessing rests upon it even if it be successful. Throw your whole energy into the pursuance of the calling you have chosen. Serve the Lord and keep Him always before you; toward men be amiable, accommodating and modest, and you will fare well even without riches. My last word to you is: Honor your mother. Help her bear her dreary widowhood. Leave her undisturbed in the use of the small estate, and assist if there should be want.

Farewell, wife and children!

Another point, children. I know well you could not, if you would, practice Judaism according to my views and as I practiced it. But remain Jews and live as Jews in the best manner of your time, not only for yourself, but also where it is meet to further the whole.

PRESIDENT GERSTLEY'S ADDRESS, DELIVERED AT THE DEDICATION OF THE PRESENT TEMPLE, JUNE 11, 1891.

LADIES AND GENTLEMEN : An occasion like the present, the dedication of a new house of worship, though awaking in some thoughtful and earnest reflections, is generally regarded by most of those present with more than ordinarily cheerful, pleasant and friendly feelings. The fact that this congregation, after years of patient struggle, has succeeded in erecting this splendid edifice for its permanent use, is not the only thought that gratifies us to-day. We are equally gratified by the thought that in the pursuit and the final accomplishment of our own difficult task, we furnish an example to those engaged in similar undertakings never to cease their endeavors until all obstacles are overcome, and their efforts crowned with success.

Small, indeed, was the beginning ; dim and dark the prospect for a speedy or even a remote success, when on the third day of October, 1847, a little band of men, scarcely more than a score in number, the pioneers, the vanguard of the now numerous Jewish inhabitants of this city, formed the first Jewish congregation of the great Northwest of this continent, naming it Kehilath Ansche Mayriv, which signifies "The Congregation of the Men of the West." They aimed to uphold and to practice the rules and precepts of the old persuasion in which they had been educated, and to which they were prompted by their own innate convictions. With no help save their indomitable energy, with means too limited to reckon on any perceptible assistance from that source, they depended mainly upon their untiring earnestness and perseverance. They formed and adopted a constitution, elected their officers, with M. L. Leopold as President, Abraham Kohn as Vice-President and Treasurer, and Philip Neuburg as Secretary. They called Rev. Ignatz Kunreuther of New York City, a profound student of Hebrew lore, to become their spiritual guide.

As a Jewish community they realized the propriety of having their own burial ground, where they and their kindred, when called hence, might find a quiet and peaceful resting place. A Jewish Burying Ground Society, which had procured about one acre of ground near the city cemetery from the City Council, was then already in existence. In sympathy with the undertaking of the newly organized congregation, they ceded their right and title in the burying ground to the congregation, which accepted it and assumed its care for the future.

They rented a loft at the southwest corner of Lake and Wells streets, near Fifth Avenue, in which to hold their services on the day of rest, as well as for other meetings. Through the influx of new-comers, who desired to inprove their condition by coming to what was then considered the far West, the membership was considerably increased, and they had to seek a more suitable location and more commodious quarters. In 1849 a lot on South Clark Street, near Quincy, was leased for five years, and a wooden stucture erected thereon to be used as a house of worship. In the fall of the same year, Rev. Dr. S. M. Isaacs of New York, was invited to assist in the dedication of the first Jewish house of worship in this city. As a result of its constant increase and activity the congregation purchased in 1854 the northeast corner of Adams and Wells streets, moved their building from Clark Street upon it, and built a basement under it to be used for school and meeting rooms.

In 1855 the congregation received a special charter from the legislature as a religious congregation.

It was in 1856 that the members came to the conclusion that the burying ground near the city cemetery would no longer answer its purpose. The sand was continually being blown in from the lake shore, so that the graves became completely covered, and in many instances relatives or friends could not find the spot where their beloved ones rested. A piece of ground in the town of Lake View, at the corner of Green Bay Road (now North Clark Street) and Belmont Avenue, containing about four acres, was then bought. It was inclosed and laid out in family lots for a cemetery. Hither were removed the bodies from the first cemetery, which was then abandoned, and subsequently, in 1882, sold to the Lincoln Park Commissioners. This, our first cemetery, now forms a part of Lincoln Park.

The congregation numbered, in 1860, 107 members or families. A new leaf was now to be turned, a new dawn to break upon the congregation, bringing with it the prospect of a more promising future. In 1861 the learned Rabbi and scholar, Rev. Dr. Liebman Adler of Detroit, Michigan, whose renown as a practical thinker preceded his coming, accepted a call from this congregation to become its spiritual leader and to direct the ethical and intellectual development of its children.   Through the scholarly attainments of the new teacher, the minds of his pupils were quickened and their desire for information encouraged.   While his pulpit utterances won for him the sympathy and affection of his hearers, his erudition commanded their attention and respect.

It was at this period, strange as it may seem, that an event took place in the history of the congregation which was as perplexing as it was remarkable.   The spirit of inquiry, of liberal thought and of doubt, seized a number of our members, who now desired a change of ritual, or, in other words, a change from the old school to the new school of reform.   Inasmuch as a majority of the members were not inclined to yield to such an innovation, as a consequence, toward the close of 1861, twenty-six of our members withdrew from the congregation.   Undaunted by such an unexpected occurrence, undismayed by the loss of some of the brighter and more liberal supporters of the congregation, the members worked with renewed vigor and more unanimity.   The congregation soon gained sufficiently in members to enable it to secure a more desirable location. In 1868 the congregation purchased the northwest corner of Wabash Avenue and Peck Court, with church buildings upon it.   With the occupancy of these new quarters came a change in our form of service, such as the introduction of an organ, choir and other more modern practices, which all added to the satisfaction of our members.

But the course of events does not always run as smoothly as we expect or as we desire.   At the second great fire of July, 1874, our church building was destroyed, and the congregation was now houseless and homeless.   Through the generosity of the trustees of the Methodist Episcopal Church, corner of Wabash Avenue and Fourteenth Street, this congregation was permitted to meet and hold its usual service on the Sabbath of the decalogue.   This brotherly kindness will always be gratefully remembered by the members of Kehilath Anshe Mayriv.

In December, 1874, the congregation purchased a lot and church building from the members of Plymouth Church, at the southeast corner of Indiana Avenue and Twenty-sixth Street, and immediately occupied the same.   The Wabash Avenue property was then sold.

On the 5th day of December, 1882, the members, with unanimous consent, voted for their esteemed minister, Rev. Dr. Adler, after his retirement from active service, a liberal stipend, a settled annuity, and a life policy, as an acknowledgment of the valuable services rendered this congregation while in charge of its affairs, although no previous promise or agreement to that effect had been made.

We deem it also proper to mention that, owing to the increase of membership, our main hall became insufficient to accommodate the immense audiences on our special holidays. The trustees of Emanuel Baptist Church, on Michigan Avenue, near Twenty-third Street, permitted this congregation to meet in their splendid edifice for the purpose of holding services on such occasions. We gratefully acknowledge their kindness and courtesy.

The town of Lake View, in which our cemetery was located, made such rapid strides and increased so quickly in population that the congregation found it unpleasant for itself, as well as annoying to the neighbors, to have their cemetery amidst so densely settled a community. It was here, in the year 1888, that one of our oldest and most generous members, widely known for his many charitable and benevolent deeds, came to the rescue. He donated twenty acres of ground near Dunning Station, in the town of Jefferson, to the congregation, with the proviso that it be improved and used as a cemetery. This generous offer was highly appreciated and gratefully accepted, and the kindness of the liberal donor acknowledged by the congregation. The ground was properly inclosed, laid out in family lots, improved, and used as a cemetery. The Lake View cemetery was abandoned and the property subsequently sold.

In 1889 the congregation secured the ground upon which this building was erected. Our property on Indiana Avenue and Twenty-sixth Street was sold to a sister congregation. In a true spirit of thoughtful kindness the president and trustees of Sinai Congregation tendered us the use of their temple, in which to hold our usual services on the historical Sabbath, until our new home be ready for occupancy. In accepting this kind invitation, this congregation expressed its appreciation of their friendly action, and avowed its willingness, at any time, to reciprocate the courtesy shown by Sinai, as well as other congregations.

The growth of the city and the change of localities caused many members to withdraw from this congregation. Among others, four flourishing sister congregations, the leaders of which were formerly members of this, the mother congregation, are now established in various sections of the city. All of them have our good will and best wishes.

After an occasional change of ministers we find in the Rev. Dr. I. S. Moses, our present rabbi, a ripe scholar, a splendid lecturer, of deep research, and one in every respect capable of directing the moral and intellectual training of our youth. His addresses are always interesting and instructive, and are listened to by numerous and attentive hearers. Our Sabbath school comprises about 100 scholars. The ethical and historical lessons taught here are designed to promote the intellectual growth of the pupils. We number to-day 194 members or heads of families. If quoted as other denominations compute their communicants, we would number between five and six hundred members.

The ground whereon this temple is built required an outlay of $36,000. The building of this edifice, including organ, pews, carpets, gas fixtures and other furnishings, cost about $110,000. After the distribution of the pews among the members, the congregation will be free from debt. All of this has been accomplished without one iota of expense to any individual member. This temple was planed and erected under the superintendence of the well-known architects, Adler & Sullivan. It has 190 pews in the auditorium and 80 in the gallery, with a seating capacity for 1,500 persons.

Thus far the Lord has helped us. We acknowledge with grateful hearts the favor, the protection, of a benign providence. We trust that henceforth in visiting this temple, we shall ever be mindful of the lofty purpose for which it is designed, the elevation of our minds, the enlargement of our intelligence, and the encouragement of the desire for higher aspirations. And if perchance others, no matter what their belief or creed, should meet us within these sacred walls, may we all strive to emulate one another in the fostering of kindness and good will among men, and in trying to be convinced and to acknowledge, that we are the offspring of one parent, children of the Father of all.

כִּי חַג הַיּוֹם לָנוּ חַג חֲמִשִּׁים שָׁנָה
חַג הַיּוֹבֵל לְקָהְלַת אַנְשֵׁי מַעֲרָב;
אֶל בֵּית אֵל הַיּוֹם יָבֹאוּ בִּרְנָנָה
מֵאִישׁ שָׂד אִשָּׁה וּמִנַּעַר עַד שָׂב.

הֵן אַךְ מִצְעָר וְכִיעַט הָיְתָה רֵאשִׁיתָהּ
וַתִּגְדַּל לִמְאוֹד וַתִּפְרַן וַתַּעַל;
כִּי אַתָּה אֵל שַׁדַּי אוֹתָהּ נָחִיתָ
בַּאֲמִתְּךָ וּבְאוֹרְךָ כְּמֵרוֹצֵי כַּעַל.

לָכֵן הַיּוֹם אֵל צוּרָה וְכִישַׂנֵּבָה
אֵת שִׁכְךָ הִיא תַעֲלֶה עַל רֹאשׁ שִׂמְחָתָהּ;
חַסְדְּךָ הַגָּדוֹל אַהֲבָתְךָ הָרַבָּה
בְּזִמְרוֹת בֶּן־יִשַׁי הֵם כָּל שִׁירָתָהּ.

כִּיהֲרֵי הַכִּנּוֹר רִנָתָם יַגְבִּירוּ
עַל כַּנְפֵי רוּחַ הַשִּׁירִים נִשָּׂאִים;
כָּל רִגְשֵׁי קֹדֶשׁ בְּנֶפֶשׁ יָעִירוּ
גַּם עָמְק עָמְק אֶל הַלֵּב הֵם בָּאִים.

יִשְׂרָאֵל עַם נֵצַח עַם אוֹהֵב אוֹר
וּבְאוֹר תּוֹרַת־אֱמֶת הֵן בֶּטַח דַּרְכֵּהוּ;
וּלְאַנְשֵׁי הַמַּעֲרָב פֹּה אֶרֶץ הַדְּרוֹר
כְּמֵרוֹצָיו אֵל נָאוֹר יִשְׁלַח אוֹרֵהוּ.

קוֹל כִּנּוֹר בֶּן־יִשַׁי יֶהֱמֶה יָרִיעַ
עַד גּוֹיִם רַבִּים רִנָתוּ יִשְׁמָעוּ;
עַד שֶׁמֶשׁ הַצְּדָקָה בַּתֵּבֵל תּוֹפִיעַ
וּבְשֵׁם אַחִים כָּל   הָעַמִּים יִקְרָאוּ.

בֵּין אַרְזֵי הַלְּבָנוֹן פִּרְחֵי הַשָּׁרוֹן
יַעַר כֵּי הַיַּרְדֵּן הַהוֹלְכִים וּכְפֵבִים ׃
בֵּין עַרְבוֹת הַבְּשָׁם קוֹל עָרֵב יָרֹן
קוֹל רִנָּה וִישׁוּעָה כֻּלּוֹ מַמְתַּקִּים ׃

וּבְכָל אַפְסֵי אֶרֶץ אִיֵּי מֶרְחַקִּים
מִמִּזְרַח שֶׁמֶשׁ יַעַד בּוֹאוּ הַיָּמָּה ׃
יֶשׁ קוֹל תַּחֲנוּנִים קוֹרֵא כְּמַעֲמַקִּים
קוֹל כִּנּוֹר בֶּן־יִשַׁי נִשְׁמַע גַּם שָׁמָּה ׃

הַקּוֹל קוֹל יַעֲקֹב קוֹל רִנָּה וּתְפִלָּה
וּבְמִזְמוֹרֵי דָוִד יַעַל הַנְּגִינוֹת ׃
אֵל צוּרוֹ הוּא נוֹתֵן יֶשְׁבַּח וּתְהִלָּה
מִצָּפוֹן כִּדָרוֹם כְּכָל הַמְּדִינוֹת ׃

כִּי עוֹד הַבַּת יַעֲקֹב אֱמוּנִים שׁוֹמֶרֶת
אַחֲרֵי יָמִים רַבִּים וּשְׁנוֹת אֲלָפִים ׃
עוֹד שַׁלְהֶבֶת־יָה בְּלִבְכָה בּוֹעֶרֶת
יַעֲרֵי יַעַד לֹא תִשְׁכַּח גּוֹאֲלָהּ בַּשָּׁמַיִם ׃

וּבָאָרֶץ הַחֲדָשָׁה בִּקְצוֹת עֵבֶר יָם
בִּגְבוּל אֶלִינַאיז שֶׁיַּקְנֶה הָעִיר ׃
קוֹל זִמְרַת־יָהּ נִשְׁמַע קוֹל גָּדוֹל וָרָם
לַמְנַצֵּחַ מִזְמוֹר עַל־עֲלָמוֹת הַשִּׁיר ׃

חִשַּׁרְתָּ כֵּי כְּשֶׁגַּן מַיִם כַּבִּירִים
יֶהֱמוּ גַּם יַחְבְּרוּ יָרִימוּ אֶת הֲמוֹנָם ׃
קוֹל יַעַל הַמַּיִם קוֹל זִמְרָה וְשִׁירִים
קוֹל כִּנּוֹר בֶּן־יִשַׁי נַקְשִׁיב בִּשְׁאוֹנָם ׃

ממזרח שמש עד מבואו.

ממזרח שמש עד מבואו:
מהלל שם ה'
(תהלים קי"ג י'-ג')

למנצח בנגינות, מזמור שיר לכבוד חג היובל אשר חננה קהלת
אנשי מערב בשיקאגא, ביום ה' ט' חשון הרנ"ח לפ"ק ביום כלאת לה
חמישים שנה מיום הוסדה:
מאת חיים בר מיטה אליסף, המכונה

H. ELIASSOF.

קוֹל כִּנּוֹר בַּדְ־יִשַׁי מְנַעֵים הַזְּמִירוֹת
לֹא נָדַם עַת מַה הַמְנַגֵּן הַנָּעִים:
וּבְדִמְכַת לֵיל יֵעוֹר נַקְשִׁיב הַשִּׁירוֹת
בִּנְשׁוֹב רוּחַ קָרִים מִבֵּין הָעֳפָאִים.

פַּעַם הַמֵּיתָרִים יֶהֱמוּ כַחֲלִילִים
כְּקַשְׁתְּ־רוּחַ תִּבְכֶּה שָׁם בְּמִסְתָּרִים:
כְּהִתְחַנֵּן אוֹבְדִים עֲתִירָתָם מְפִילִים
לִפְנֵי כֵס אֵל רַחוּם שָׁם כֵּן הַמְּצָרִים.

וּפַעַם יָרִיכוּ קוֹל עֲנוֹת הַגְּבוּרָה
וּבְקוֹלוֹ הֵיּדָד אָז יַעֲנֶה הַר הֶהָרִים:
כִּתְרוּעַת עַם מוּרָט לִקְרַאת הַבְּשׂוֹרָה
כִּי גָבַר עַל אוֹיֵב נָפְלוּ הַצָּרִים.

הַכְּזֶמֶר בְּלֵיל יַעֲלֵי כְּעֵין גַּנִּים
אָז יָשִׁיר שִׁירַת דּוֹדִים בֵּין הַנְּטָעִים:
הַשִּׁירִים נוֹתְנִים לַנֶּפֶשׁ כְּעֵדָנִים
וּבַלֵּב יָעִירוּ שַׂרְעַפִּים נִשָּׂאִים.

אַ

"From the Rising of the Sun Unto the Going Down of the Same."*

From the rising of the sun unto the going down of the same the Lord's name be praised. Psalms cxiii, 3.

To the chief musician on Neginoth, a Psalm of song, in honor of the golden jubilee, celebrated by Kehillath Anshe Maarabb of Chicago, Thursday, November 4, 1897.

The psalmist's voice in death is stilled;
The minstrel sleeps in royal mound;
His harp is still with music filled,
In stilly night we hear its sound.

At times the strings despair express,
As women weep, in sorrow moan;
As anguished souls in dire distress
A prayer send to mercy's throne.

In triumph's strains they oft break out,
From crest and crag an echo rings,
As rolls a nation's joyous shout
To welcome him who freedom brings.

The nightingale at garden rills
Then sings of love the sweetest notes;
The song our soul with rapture thrills
And fills the mind with lofty thoughts.

Where cedars high and mighty grow.
Where Sharon's roses wand'rers greet;
Where Jordan's waters roll and flow
The harp resounds in cadence sweet.

On isles remote, on distant shores,
From sunny south to western clime,
A praying voice entreats, implores,
There sounds the harp's enchanting rhyme.

The voice is Jacob's song of praise.
Of Israel's dispersed who never tire
Their hearts to God in chants to raise.
In psalmist's songs on lute and lyre.

For Judah's sons are still the same,
Though ages passed in rushing flight;
They still adore God's holy name,
And true remain to Heaven's light.

The western world's all glorious crown,
Where freedom's brilliant gems abound,
Chicago holds and calls its own,
And there today we hear the sound.

And mighty Michigan is stirred,
Its waters rush and surge and foam;
The psalmist's harp above is heard,
Its strains ascend to heaven's dome.

For Maarabh's men who consecrate
Their lives, O God, to truth and Thee,
Today devoutly celebrate
In joy their Golden Jubilee.

Though weak and small they then appeared,
They gained in strength and rose and spread;
They onward marched and never feared,
For truth and light their feet had led.

O God, our Lord and King above!
Today their thanks they gladly bring;
Thy kindness great, Thy boundless love
In David's psalms with joy they sing.

The east wind spreads its sailing wings,
The harp in song reverberates,
Through heart and soul the music rings,
Into their depths it penetrates.

O Israel! O name immortal, proud!
O law of truth our strength and might!
In freedom's land now pray aloud
We Maarabh men for Heaven's light.

O psalmist's harp awake! awake!
And play thy lay of earnest mood,
Until new dawn for mankind break
And nations live in brotherhood.

---

*The author's free translation from the original Hebrew.

KEHILLATH ANSHE MAYRIV,

Aaron, J.,
Adler, Dankmar,
Adler, Elias,
Adler, Lewis.
Adler, Morris,
Adler, Philip,
Alexander, Philip,
Auerbach, J. C.,
Auerbach S ,
Austrian, Joseph,
Austrian, Sal.,
Axman, David,
Bach, Emanuel,
Bach, L.,
Bacharach, Sam,
Baer, Philip,
Baker, Moses,
Barbe, B.,
Barnett, Henry.
Barth, Alexander.
Bauland, Henry,
Bauland, Isaac,
Bauland, Jacob H.,
Bauland, Jos. H.,
Bauland, Morris,
Bear, R.,
Beiersdorf, L.,
Beiersdorf, R.,
Benjamin, Henry.
Benjamin, Jacob,
Benjamin, Louis,
Berg, Henry,
Bernheim, Jacob,
Bettman, Samuel.
Biers, M.,
Bloch, Simon,
Block, Isaac,
Bloom, Moses,
Boskowitz, A.,
Braham, Geo.,
Brede, David,
Brill, A.,
Brownsbild, M.,
Brucker, Henry.
Brunneman, B.,
Brunswick, Charles,
Brunswick, Emanuel,
Brunswick, Joseph,
Byer, P.,

Cahn, Henry,
Cahn, Jacob L.,
Cahn, Leopold,
Cantrowitz, S.,
Cassman, A.,
Cerf, Dr.,
Childs, Jos. N.,
Clayburgh, Martin.
Cline, Jacob,
Cline, Levy,
Cohen, Abraham,
Cohen, Lewis,
Cohen, Michael,
Cohen, M.,
Cohen, Mendel A.,
Cohn, W.,
Cole, Henry,
Cole, Sam,
Cook, Jessel,
Cossman, A.,
Cowen, Israel,
Daube, Aaron,
D'Ancona, Abm.,
Daniels, M.,
Danziger, Adolph,
Dernburg, Carl,
Dernhaim, M.,
Despres, Alfred,
Despres, Cerf,
Dessauer, Isaac.
Dreshfeld, M.,
Dubetz, Samuel,
Ederheimer, Max,
Einstein, Joseph,
Einstein, B.,
Einstein, George,
Einstein, Morris,
Eisendrath, B. D.,
Eisendrath, Benjamin,
Eisendrath, Cushman,
Eisendrath, Levy,
Eisendrath, Louis,
Eisendrath, Nathan,
Eisenstaedt, Isidor,
Eisenstaedt, Rudolph,
Eliassof, Herman,
Epstein, Nathan,
Ettlinger, Henry.
Falk, Herman B.,

Falk, M. L.,
Fass, Chas.,
Fass, J.,
Fass, Jacob,
Feibelman, A. L.,
Fernberg, Sal,
Fernberg, Saml,
Fichtenberg, M.,
Fish, David,
Fish, L ,
Fish, Sol T.,
Fleishman, Henry.
Fleishman, M. S.,
Foreman, B.,
Foreman, G.,
Foreman, Henry,
Foreman, Isaac,
Foreman, Rudolph,
Frank, A.,
Frank, David,
Frank, Emanuel,
Frank, Joseph,
Frankel, A. B.,
Frankenthal, E.,
Franklin, Simon,
Freiberger, L. H.,
Freind, A.,
Freind, Chas.,
Freind, Feit,
Freind, Nathan,
Freshman, A.,
Friedman, L.,
Friedman, William,
Friesleben, Isaac,
Friesleben, L.,
Fuller, Jacob,
Geisman, Saloman,
Gelder, Isaac,
Gelder, Jonas,
Gerstley, Henry,
Gerstley, M. M.,
Glaser, Max,
Glick, Lepman,
Glueckauf, S.,
Goldberg, N. D.,
Goldenberg, Jonas,
Goldman, Max,
Goldsmith, Henry,
Goldsmith, Moses,

Goldstein, S.,
Goodkind, B.,
Goodkind, Edward,
Goodkind, Lewis,
Goodman, Emanuel,
Goodman, Magnus,
Gottlove, John,
Greenebaum, Elias,
Greenebaum, Henry,
Greenebaum, Isaac,
Greenebaum, Jacob, Sr.,
Greenebaum, Jacob, Jr.,
Greenebaum, J. M.,
Greenebaum, Leon,
Greenebaum, Michael,
Gruen, J. J.,
Guthman, Ed.
Haas, Henry S.,
Haas, Joseph,
Hamburger, Sol,
Harris, S.,
Hart, Henry N.,
Hasterlik, Chas.,
Hasterlik, Simon,
Heilbron, Jonas,
Heilbron Louis,
Heilbroner, S.,
Heine, H. M.,
Heller, Leo L.,
Herman, Daniel,
Herman, Henry,
Herzog, Anton,
Herzog, Ignatz,
Hess, Adolph,
Hess, Emanuel,
Hess, Isaac,
Hess, Jacob,
Hess, Lipman,
Hess, Siegel,
Hirsch, Jacob,
Hirsch, Moses,
Hirsch, Salomon,
Hirsch, Salomon,
Hirschman, Henry,
Hofheimer, A.,
Hofman, M.,
Honigsberger, A.,
Horner, Emil,
Horner, Henry,
Horner, Joseph,
Hyman, Feit,
Hyman, Geo. S.,
Hyman, Henry,
Hyman, Sig.,
Isaacs, M. C.,
Israel, Max,
Jacobs, E.,
Jacobs, Myer,

Jackson, Julius,
Jaros, Jacob,
Jessel, Edw. A.,
Jessel, G. A.,
Jones, Isaac,
Kahn, Jacob,
Karger, Simon,
Kaiser, Sal.,
Katz, J. P.,
Katzauer, Isaac,
Kaufman, Benjamin,
Keefer, L.,
Klein, Gustav L.,
Klein, Simon,
Kleinert, A.,
Kling, Moses,
Kohn, Abraham,
Kohn, A. Sr.,
Kohn, A.,
Kohn, A. H.,
Kohn, D. A.,
Kohn, H. A.,
Kohn, Hirsch,
Kohn, Isaac A.,
Kohn, Jos. A.,
Kohn, Morris,
Kohn, Simon H.,
Kramer, N.,
Krohn, Jacob,
Kuh, Oscar N.,
Kunreuther, Ignatz,
Landsburg, M.,
Lederer, Emanuel,
Leopold, Aaron F.,
Leopold, Asar F.,
Leopold, Henry,
Leopold, H. F.,
Leopold, L. F.,
Leopold, Lewis,
Leopold, L. M.,
Lepman, Louis,
Loewenberg, Isaac,
Loewenstein, S.,
Levi, Abraham,
Levi, D.,
Levi, Sal. A.,
Levi, Salomon,
Levy, Abraham,
Liebenstein, Abrm.,
Liebenstein, Henry
Liebenstein, Joseph,
Liebenstein, Sal.,
Lieberman, R.,
Lindauer, B.,
Lindauer, Max,
Lindauer, Seligman,
Livingston, S.,
Lobstein, Samuel,

Loeb, Jacob,
Loebe, E.,
Loebe, M.,
Lowenthal, B.,
Louis, A.,
Lucky, Isaac,
Lyons, Henry E.,
Maas, Frederick,
Mandel, Leon,
Mandelbaum, M. H.,
Manheimer Gottfried,
Marcus, Isidor,
Marcus, Solms,
Marienthal, George,
Marks, S.,
Markwald, Bernhard,
May, Jacob,
May, Sigmund,
Mayer, Aaron,
Mayer, David,
Mayer, Fred,
Mayer, Henry,
Mayer, Lemle,
Mayer, Leopold,
Mayer, Louis,
Mayer, M.,
Mayer, Samuel,
Mayer, Simon,
Mayers, Chas. J.,
Meyer, Henry,
Meyers, J. H.,
Myers, Simon,
Moses, Albert,
Moss, Myer,
Moyses, Emanuel,
Nast, David,
Nessler, S. C.,
Neuberger, Chas,
Neuberger, Phil
Neumann, Ignatz,
Neuman, S.,
Newberger, Mayer,
Newmann, J. Jr.,
Newman, Maier,
Oplatky, Joseph,
Oppenheim, M J.,
Oppenheimer, Moses,
Oswald, Ph.,
Paretz, Joseph,
Pfaelzer, David J.,
Pfaelzer, David M.,
Pfaelzer, Simon,
Phillipsborn, Max,
Peiser, M.,
Peiser, Samuel,
Petersberger, Emil,
Pincus, Ephraim,
Polachek, Leo,

PRESENT MEMBERS.

Pollak, Henry,
Pollak, Joseph,
Powel, S.,
Regensburg, Henry,
Reinemann, Moses,
Rosenberg, Benjamin,
Rosenberg, Jacob,
Rosenberg, Julius,
Rosenberg, Wm.,
Rosenfeld, Henry,
Rosenfeld, I.,
Rosenfeld, Levy,
Rosenfield, M.,
Rosenfeld, Wolf.
Rosenfels, S.,
Rosenheim, D.,
Rosenstock, J.,
Rosenthal, B.,
Rosenthal, H. S.,
Rosenthal, S.,
Rothschild, Joseph,
Rothschild, Leopold,
Rothschild, Max M.,
Rubel, Abraham,
Rubel, G.,
Rubel, Isaac,
Rubovits, A.,
Salomon, J. J.,
Salomon, S.,
Salomon, Wolf.
Samson, David,
Schlesinger, George,
Schlesinger, S.,
Schlossman, B.,
Schlossman, Joseph,
Schlossman, Samuel,
Schnadig, Jacob.
Schnadig, Jos. M.,
Schoneman, B.,
Schwabacher, Henry,
Selig, G ,
Schaefer, Wolff.

Scheierman, A ,
Shield, L. D.,
Schiff, A.,
Schmaltz, Jos.,
Shoninger, B.,
Shottenfels, S.,
Shubert, B.,
Schwab, Chas. H.,
Schwarzchild, S.,
Silverman, Geo.,
Silverman, Lazarus,
Silberman, Sigmund.
Simon, Henry,
Singer, Morris D.,
Simpson, W. M.,
Smith, Aaron,
Smith, Benjamin Jacob,
Smith, Morris,
Snydacker, G.,
Soudheim, B.,
Soudheimer, E.,
Spiegel, Jos.,
Spiegel, Moses,
Spiegel, Sal.,
Spitz, Samuel,
Stein, Chas.,
Stein, Joseph,
Stein, L. D.,
Stein, Sal.,
Stein, Sigmund,
Steiner, Henry,
Steiner, Jacob.
Stern, Anson,
Stern, B.,
Stettauer, Abraham,
Stettauer, David,
Stiefel, S.,
Stransky, E. J.,
Straus, J. W.,
Strauss, L.,
Straus, Nathan,
Straus, Samuel.

Strauss, Jacob N.,
Strauss, Julius,
Straus, Sol.,
Straus, W.,
Strelitz, S.,
Swiskey, H.,
Tallert, Henry,
Theobald, J. H.,
Trauerman, Jos. L.,
Ullman, Moses,
Undermayer, David,
Vogel, Abraham,
Vogel, Chas.,
Waller, Morris,
Ware, Oscar W.,
Wasserman, D.,
Weigselbaum, M.,
Weil, Marcus,
Weil, Moses,
Weil, Solomon,
Weinberg, M.,
Weineman, Martin,
Weineman, Max,
Weinstein, Samuel,
Weisel, Jos.,
Wendel, Chas.,
Wetzler, Chas.,
Wheeler, M.,
Wilzinsky, A.,
Windmuller, L.,
Wirmisky, A.,
Witkowsky, D.,
Wolf, Bernard,
Wolf, Isaac,
Wolf, Salomon,
Wolff, Simon,
Wolfner, Isaac,
Wormser, David,
Wormser, Isaac,
Wurzburger, L.,
Yondorf, Simon,
Ziegler, Isaac.

WIDOW MEMBERS.

Mrs. J. Bernheimer,
Mrs. S. Cole,
Mrs H. Cole,
Mrs M. Clayburgh,
Mrs. Fleishman,
Mrs. W. Friedman,
Mrs. H. Falk,
Mrs. Eliza Frank,
Mrs. J. Goldenburg,
Mrs. H. Hirshman,
Mrs. Herzog,

Mrs. L. Hess,
Mrs. H. Horner,
Mrs. E. Horner,
Mrs. Kling,
Mrs. A. Kohn,
Mrs. L. F. Leopold,
Mrs. A· F. Leopold,
Mrs. Louis Leopold,
Mrs. H. F. Leopold,
Mrs. Louis Lepman,
Mrs. E. Loeb,

Mrs. Loebstein,
Mrs. H. Mayer,
Mrs. Jacob May,
Mrs. Daniel Nast,
Mrs. M. Peiser,
Mrs. W. Rosenfield,
Mrs. M. Rothschild,
Mrs. S. Schmalz,
Mrs. H. Steiner,
Mrs. H. Tallert,
Mrs. S. Weil.

ASSOCIATE MEMBERS.

Eisenstaedt, Leo.   Guettel, Jos.,   Moog, David,
Houseman, M. M.,   Jackson, Simon.

TO THE READER.

It would be more than improper if I should adorn myself with feathers which really do not belong to me. Considering this, and furthermore considering that honors should be rendered to the man to whom honor is due, I beg to state here that by far the larger share of the labor in gathering the material for the present monograph and preparing the same for the press, has been done by my friend, Mr. H. Eliassof. A few weeks ago I was officially requested by a committee of K. A. M. to write such a monograph and to have it published prior to the rapidly approaching Semi-Centennial of the congregation. To this flattering request I answered that the time was too short in which to collect, to examine and to sift thoroughly all the necessary material and to bring it in proper shape. I was then told that Mr. Eliassof, the principal of the Sabbath School of K. A. M., should be my collaborator and that he would undertake the collection of the historical data, etc., and the suggestion was added that otherwise we might work jointly together. Upon these conditions I consented. I now bear witness that, with a rare faithfulness and devotedness to his work, Mr. Eliassof examined the records, letters and other papers still extant in the archives of the congregation and made the proper extracts therefrom; that he interviewed several older members of the congregation and other persons living here; that by correspondence with persons now residing outside of Chicago he elicited some valuable information; and that by so doing a rich material was brought together. Not all of it could be made use of. Much of it could not be used on account of its being not important enough, or of its being not sufficiently verified. For other information used herein, which was received by the kindness of various parties, hereby our thanks are expressed. The manuscript prepared by my friend was read by me, and as far as possible I collated carefully the facts mentioned with the original sources. So much, then, I believe, I can safely say, that at least the real facts, as related here, have been ascertained to be true, and that of the strictly historical parts of this essay it can be maintained that they are reliable. In consequencee of the brevity of the time at our command, it is likely that a few minor points may have been overlooked, or that some slight inaccuracies may have crept in. If this should be the case, the kind reader will grant us indulgence.

B. FELSENTHAL.

CHICAGO, October 28, 1897.

www.ingramcontent.com/pod-product-compliance
Lightning Source LLC
Chambersburg PA
CBHW030615270326
41927CB00007B/1185